KOREAN

한국어

Maji Rhee 著

HAKUEISHA

Contents

Acknowledgments

Welcome to the world of the Korean language! There are growing numbers of fans of K-Pop, K-Cosmetics, and K-Cinema fanning interest in the Korean language. "K-razy" as a journalist Kathleen Beckett (Nov. 27, 2021, NY Times) noted, the South Korean TV series Squid Game has become Netflix's most-watched show, and people are trying to learn dance like K-pop stars.

We will begin learning the Korean alphabet, *Hangeul* which is a writing system created by King Sejong in 1443. Subsequent lessons include basic dialogues and fundamentals which will enable students to speak core spoken phrases followed by drills and use exercises.

This textbook covers themes related to learning names of the days of the week, colors, names of family members, and objects which are based on the ACTFL (American Council on Teaching of Foreign Languages) novice and intermediate level standards. Each lesson is organized into five parts: Basic dialogue, vocabulary, grammar, practice, and utilization. Each lesson introduces basic dialogue, vocabulary, grammar patterns, practice sentences, and utilization questions based on the dialogues.

At the end of each lesson, you will communicate with phrases used in common informal settings in daily life. Also, cultural words particular to the Korean language are introduced. Please note that topics related to politically incorrect questions are not included. Exercise questions do not include asking a person about friends of an opposite gender or alcohol-related content.

The author and the members at the Lingua Franca Zeminar at Waseda University would like to express our sincere appreciation to students and colleagues for their constructive comments and encouragement. Our gratitule extends to President Byung-min Song at Hakueisha. And, the author's special thanks to Ms. Sunkyoung Kim for her valuable editorial advice.

Author

M.J.R.

Tokyo, Japan

2023

A Short Story of the Korean Language

Welcome to the Korean language! While learning Korean, you will have a chance to compare Korean with your own native language. By comparing, you have an opportunity to observe your own native language from a third perspective. A native language is often projected when learning a target language. For instance, in conversational Korean, the first person singular, "I" is usually omitted. For speakers of English, zero reference or no reference to "I" or the second person singular "you" would be awkward. You might feel that you need a subject to be stated. One of the common examples is stating the subject "I." For instance, "I had lunch" in Korean would be "had lunch". This means, in conversational Korean, the speaker "I" is usually omitted.

The Korean language does not have a gender marker such as in "*le livre*" the book or "*la voiture*" which means the automobile, in French. In Korean, nouns are not gendered. Here are several points of comparison.

(1) Korean is a phonetic language, not a tonal language. The Korean writing system is based on the combination of vowels and consonants. Once a person recognizes 14 vowels and consonants, reading can be achieved in a fairly short period of time.

(2) Highly developed verb endings is one common characteristic. The dictionary form of a verb or the verb stem remains unchanged. Affixed conjugation is the linguistic term for such a pattern.

공부하다	Dictionary form: To study
공부하세요.	Please study.
공부하지요	He/she is studying, isn't he/she studying? (hedging/tag)
공부하면	If I study
공부하겠어요.	Would/will you study?
공부하시지 않으시겠어요?	Would you not study?

(3) Nouns in Korean, unlike French or German, have no cases and are not gendered.

(4) Presence of honorifics and polite speech styles: There are formal, informal polite, and blunt forms. Formal or informal polite endings are usually used when conversing with your Korean colleagues or acquaintance. A blunt form is used when talking with a close friend or a younger person.

읽다.	Dictionary form: To read
읽으십니다.	Formal polite + honorific infix
읽습니다.	Formal polite -ㅂ/습니다
읽어요.	Informal polite -어/아 요
읽어.	Blunt form dropping 요

(5) More than sixty percent of Korean nouns derive from Chinese characters. For example, 대학교 (大學校) can be converted into Chinese characters. Nouns that cannot be converted into Chinese characters are "pure Korean words."

(6) Sentence word order is Subject - Object - Verb

Word order in Korean
Subject - Subject particle - Verb
Subject - Object - Object particle - Verb

띄어쓰기	띄어쓰기	
spacing	spacing	
저는	대학생	입니다.
Subject subject particle	Noun	Verb Copula
I	college student	am.

New Romanization in Hangeul

This book introduces New Romanization in *Hangeul* to facilitate recognizing syllables, orthography, and help learners to begin reading in Korean.

The Ministry of Culture and Tourism (MoCT) of the Republic of Korea formally proclaimed a new system of Romanization for the Korean Language in 2000. When romanizing personal names or geographical names, the usage of the new romanization is suggested. In this book, the new romanization system published by National Institute of Korean Language, Republic of Korea is used.

New Romanization System

1 Basic vowels and double vowels

ㅏ	ㅓ	ㅗ	ㅜ	ㅡ	ㅣ	ㅐ	ㅔ	ㅚ	ㅟ	ㅑ	ㅕ	ㅛ	ㅠ	ㅒ	ㅖ	ㅘ	ㅙ	ㅝ	ㅞ	ㅢ
a	eo	o	u	eu	i	ae	e	oe	wi	ya	yeo	yo	yu	yae	ye	wa	wae	wo	we	ui

2 Romanization of consonants

Plain	ㄱ	ㄴ	ㄷ	ㄹ	ㅁ	ㅂ	ㅅ	ㅇ	ㅈ
	g	n	d	r/l	m	b	s	ng	j

Aspirated	ㅊ	ㅋ	ㅌ	ㅍ	ㅎ
	ch	k	t	p	h

Tense	ㄲ	ㄸ	ㅃ	ㅆ	ㅉ
	kk	tt	pp	ss	jj

Korean Alphabet

Consonants

ㄱ ㄴ ㄷ ㄹ ㅁ ㅂ ㅅ ㅇ ㅈ ㅊ ㅋ ㅌ ㅍ ㅎ

g,k n d,t r,l m b s ng j ch k t p h

ㄲ ㄸ ㅃ ㅆ ㅉ

kk tt pp ss jj

Vowels

ㅏ ㅑ ㅓ ㅕ ㅗ ㅛ ㅜ ㅠ ㅡ ㅣ

a ya eo yeo o yo u yu eu i

ㅐ ㅒ ㅔ ㅖ ㅘ ㅙ ㅚ ㅝ ㅞ ㅟ ㅢ

ae yae e ye wa wae oe wo we wi ui

There are ten simple vowels and eleven double vowels. The vowel formulation is based on the cosmic principle of heaven, earth, and humans. The graphic signs for heaven are represented as a circular dot, earth as a horizontal line, and human as a vertical line.

There are two types of vowels based on the Yin and Yang principle. 아 and 오 are bright vowels and 어 and 우 are dark vowels. These two types of vowels will later be applied to verb conjugations based on vowel harmonization.

하늘 천 天	땅 지 地	사람 인 人
heaven	earth	human
·	—	|

Yang — *Yin*
아, 오 — 어, 우
bright vowel — dark vowel

아 — 어
rising sun in the east — sun setting in the west

오 — 우
sun rising at the horizon — sun below the horizon

이
Neutral vowel

Yang or Bright Vowels

ㅏ [a]	ㅐ [ae]	ㅑ [ya]	ㅒ [yae]	ㅗ[o]	ㅘ[wa]	ㅙ[wae]	ㅚ[oe]	ㅛ[yo]

Yin or Dark Vowels

ㅓ [oe]	ㅔ [e]	ㅕ [yeo]	ㅖ [ye]	ㅜ[u]	ㅝ[wo]	ㅞ[we]	ㅟ[wi]	ㅠ[yu]	ㅡ[eu]	ㅢ[ui]

ㅣ [i] is neutral, neither yin nor yang.

Simple vowels

아	야	어	여	오	요	우	유	으	이
a	ya	eo	yeo	o	yo	u	yu	eu	i

Double vowels

1 y + vowel 애 예
                  yae ye

2 w + vowel 와 왜 워 웨 외 위
                  wa wae wo we oe wi

3 ae 애   e 에

4 ui 의

아 + 이 -애 야 + 이 -얘 어 + 이 -에 여 + 이 -예	오 + 아 -와 오 + 애 -왜 오+ 이 -외	우 + 어 -워 우 + 에 -웨 우 + 이 -위	으+ 이 -의

Reading practice

아이	
우유	
여유	
오이	
이유	
여야	
애	애, 개, 배, 새, 해, 개미, 노래, 야채
얘	얘기
에	네, 가게, 세수
예	예, 세계, 시계

와	과자, 치과, 교과서
왜	돼지, 쾌유
외	외과, 외래어
워	워드, 타워
웨	웨하스, 웨이브
위	귀, 뒤, 취미
의	의미, 의회, 주의

Identify double vowels

개미	대학	배	재미	얘기	에너지
세계	차례	교과서	사과	화가	회화
돼지	아래	외모	회의	타워	웨하스
웨이브	위로	주사위	의뢰	의지	주의

There are fourteen simple consonants, five double consonants, and eleven consonant combinations. Basic consonants are formed in reference to pictographic representation of phonology based on the position of tongue, teeth and the shape of lips when pronouncing the consonants.

There are fourteen simple consonants:

ㄱ	ㄴ	ㄷ	ㄹ	ㅁ	ㅂ	ㅅ	ㅇ	ㅈ	ㅊ	ㅋ	ㅌ	ㅍ	ㅎ
g	n	d	l, r	m	b	s	ng	j	ch	k	t	p	h

Double consonants

ㄲ	ㄸ	ㅃ	ㅆ	ㅉ
kk	dd	pp	ss	jj

Double consonants eleven combinations:

ㄳ	ㄵ	ㅀ	ㄺ	ㄼ	ㄻ	ㄽ	ㄾ	ㅀ	ㅄ

Plain

ㄱ	ㄴ	ㄷ	ㄹ	ㅁ	ㅂ	ㅅ	ㅇ	ㅈ

Nasals (ㄴ, ㅁ, ㅇ)

ㄴ	ㅁ	ㅇ
n	m	ng

Liquids (ㄹ)

r	l

Aspirated

ㅊ	ㅋ	ㅌ	ㅍ	ㅎ

Glottalized

ㄲ	ㄸ	ㅃ	ㅆ	ㅉ

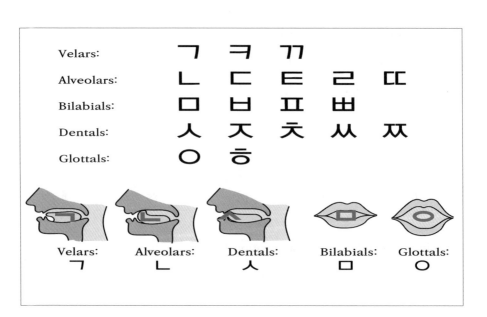

ㄱ	가구, 고기, 야구, 여기, 이야기
ㄴ	나, 나이, 누구, 누나, 어느
ㄷ	구두, 어디, 오다
ㄹ	거리, 다리, 요리, 우리
ㅁ	나무, 머리, 고구마, 어머니
ㅂ	두부, 바다, 보리, 부모, 바나나
ㅅ	교수, 버스, 수도, 소나기
ㅇ	아버지, 아이, 여우, 여유, 이유
ㅈ	모자, 바지, 저기
ㅊ	차, 주차, 치마
ㅋ	코, 크다, 크리스마스
ㅌ	도토리, 토마토
ㅍ	표, 커피, 파리, 스포츠, 피아노
ㅎ	하나, 하루, 호수
ㄲ	까치, 꼬마, 꼬리, 토끼, 까마귀
ㄸ	또, 머리띠
ㅃ	뿌리, 아빠, 오빠
ㅆ	쓰다, 아가씨, 아저씨
ㅉ	가짜, 버찌, 찌개

Batchim - An ending consonant or vowel

Korean writing is presented in syllables composed of an initial vowel or consonant, a medial vowel or consonant, and an ending called *Batchim*.

When consonants are used as a final *batchim*, they are pronounced in seven representative sounds.

Batchim ending letter	Pronunciation	
ㄱ, ㄲ, ㅋ	k	가족 밖 부엌
ㄴ	n	눈, 돈
ㄷ,ㅅ,ㅆ,ㅉ,ㅊ,ㅌ,ㅎ	t	곧, 맛, 꽃, 밭, 좋다
ㄹ	l	길, 달, 물
ㅁ	m	그림, 사람, 이름
ㅂ,ㅍ	p	밥, 입, 숲, 잎
ㅇ	ng	강, 고향, 콩

Syllable Structure

There are four patterns of syllable blocks. Each Korean syllable is made up of at least one vowel.

1   One letter syllable block: Vowel 아 야 어 여 오 우 요 으 이
                                                    애 얘 에 예 외 위 왜 워 웨

2   Two letter syllable blocks: Consonant + Vowel 교

3   Three letter syllable blocks: Consonant + Vowel + Consonant 학

4   Four letter syllable blocks: Consonant + Vowel + Consonant +
                                        Consonant 값 밝

While we are trying to recognize vowels and consonants, new romanization will help us read *Hangeul*. We will have a list of vowels and consonants, and we can begin reading syllables.

Examples

[자모별 표기]

모음

ㅏ	ㅓ	ㅗ	ㅜ	ㅡ	ㅣ	ㅐ	ㅔ	ㅚ	ㅟ
a	eo	o	u	eu	i	ae	e	oe	wi

ㅑ	ㅕ	ㅛ	ㅠ	ㅒ	ㅖ	ㅘ	ㅙ	ㅝ	ㅞ	ㅢ
ya	yeo	yo	yu	yae	ye	wa	wae	wo	we	ui

자음

ㄱ	ㄲ	ㅋ	ㄷ	ㄸ	ㅌ	ㅂ	ㅃ	ㅍ
g,k	kk	k	d,t	tt	t	b,p	pp	p

ㅈ	ㅉ	ㅊ	ㅅ	ㅆ	ㅎ	ㄴ	ㅁ	ㅇ	ㄹ
j	jj	ch	s	ss	h	n	m	ng	r,l

연습 Reading

가구 가방 가족 고양이 공책 공항 교실 극장 김치 꽃

남자 남편 냉장고 눈

달 대사관 대학교 도서관 돈 딸

라면 라디오

목 몸 문 물

바람 발 방 백화점 병원 불 비행기 빵

사람 사전 사진 산 서울 손 손수건 수박 시장 시청 시강 신문 신발

안경 약국 양말 얼굴 연필 영화 왼쪽 우산 우체국 운동 은행 이름 입 잎

자동차 전화 젓가락

창문 책 책상
──
태권도 태극기
──
편지
──
하늘 학교 한국 한국어 한글 할머니 할아버지
──

Pronunciation Rules

Unlike in English where "a" in "eat" would be differently pronounced "a" in apple, Korean vowels and consonants usually have one sound. For example, 아 would be pronounced "a." There are seven major pronunciation rules that will help you to pronounce and write Korean words.

1. Liaison

When a syllable ends with a *batchim* and is followed by a syllable that begins with a vowel, the *batchim* will be carried over. Liaison is common in French. "The children" in French is written "les enfants." When a word which ends in a consonant, the consonant is carried over or assimilated into a following vowel, and is pronounce "lezanfants." The ending consonant "s" will sounds like a "z." Similarly, 국어 which means the national language (Korean) is written as "kuk-eo." When pronounced, the third consonant ㄱ is carried over to the vowel ㅇ, and thus becomes "kugeo."

국어   국╱어

kuk eo   kugeo

읽어요   읽╱어 요

ilk eo yo   ilgeo yo

2. Consonant aspiration

Here is a list of the four patterns showing how consonants are aspirated when two particular consonants collide.

ㄱ + ㅎ → ㅋ   막히다 (to be clugged) makida   묵호 (name of the place) *Mukho*

ㅂ + ㅎ → ㅍ   입학 (entrance of a school) ippak 법학 (the study of law) beopak
집현전 (The Hall of Worthies is called *Jiphyeonjeon* where the *Hangeul* writing system was created)

ㅎ + ㄷ → ㅌ   좋다 (to be good) jota   놓다 (to place) nota

ㅎ + ㅈ → ㅊ   좋지요 (It is good, isn't it?) jochiyo

3. Pronunciation in consonant clusters

ㄱ + ㅁ/ㄴ → ㅇ   국물 (broth) gungmul

ㄷ/ㅌ + ㅁ/ㄴ → ㄴ   닫는다 (to close) danuninda   낱말 (a word) nanmal

ㅂ + ㅁ/ㄴ → ㅁ   갑니다 (going) gamnida

ㅅ + ㄴ → ㄴ   솟는다 (to spring up) sonunda

ㅆ + ㄴ → ㄴ   있는 (existing) inun

ㅈ + ㄴ → ㄴ   젖는다 (to get wet) jeonunda

ㅊ + ㄴ → ㄴ   빛난다 (shinning) binanda

ㅍ + ㅁ → ㅂ   앞문 (front door) apmum

4. The case of palatalization

The consonant ㄷ or ㅌ is followed by 이 or ㅎ, the following consonant is pronounced either ㅈ or ㅊ.

ㄷ/ㅌ → ㅈ/ㅊ

ㄷ + 이 → 지   해돋이 (sunrise) haedo<u>j</u>i

ㅌ + 이 → 치   끝이 보입니다. (The end can be seen.) kku<u>tchi</u> boinda.

ㄷ + ㅎ + 이 → 치   닫히다 (to be closed) da<u>tchi</u>da

5. Tensification

ㄱ + ㄱ	ㄲ	경복궁 (*Gyungbok* Palace)	*Gyungbokkung*
ㄷ + ㄷ	ㄸ	식당 (cafeteria)	shik<u>tt</u>ang
ㅂ + ㅂ	ㅃ	입국 (entry to a country)	ip<u>kk</u>uk
ㅂ + ㅅ	ㅆ	합숙 (lodging together)	hap<u>ss</u>uk
ㅂ + ㅈ	ㅉ	잡지 (magazine)	jap<u>jj</u>i

5. ㅎ weakening

ㅎ is weakened when the subsequent or preceding consonants collide with ㄴ or ㅇ
전화 (telephone) jeo<u>nw</u>a 번호 (number) beo<u>n</u>o 좋아요 (It is good.) jo<u>w</u>ayo

6. Assimilation

Assimilation occurs depending on adjacent consonants.

ㄱ + ㄹ → ㅇ + ㄴ 격리 (isolation) gyong<u>ni</u>

ㄴ + ㄹ → ㄴ + ㄴ 신문로 (name of a street) in Seoul *Sinmun<u>no</u>*

ㄴ + ㄹ → ㄹ + ㄹ 언론 (press) eo<u>ll</u>on

ㄹ + ㄴ → ㄹ + ㄹ 신라 (name of a dynasty in Korean history) *Silla*

ㅁ + ㄹ → ㅁ + ㄴ 심리 (psychology) sim<u>ni</u>

ㅂ + ㄹ → ㅁ + ㄴ 왕십리 (name of a place in Seoul) *Wangsim<u>ni</u>*

ㅇ + ㄹ → ㅇ + ㄴ 종로 (name of a street in Seoul) *Jong<u>no</u>*

7. Examples of different batchim but the same pronunciation

낟 (a piece) 낮 (daytime) 낫 (scythe) 낯 (face) are prounuced "nat."

빚 (debt) 빗 (comb) 빛 (light) are pronounced "bit."

앞 (front) 압 (pressure) are pronounced "ap."

잎 (leaves) 입 (mouth) are pronounced "ip."

8. Double Batchim

Pronounce only the first consonant *batchim*   ㄳ, ㅄ, ㄶ, ㄼ, ㄾ, ㅀ, ㅄ
Pronounce only the second consonant *batchim*   ㄺ, ㄻ, ㄿ

(1) ㄳ, ㄺ → k   넋 neok (soul)   닭 dak (chicken)

(2) ㄵ → n   앉다 anta (to sit)

(3) ㄶ → n   많다 manta (to be many)

     ㅀ → l   끓다 kkuilta (to boil)

(4) ㄻ → m   젊다 jeomta (to be young)

(5) ㄼ → l   넓다 neolta (to be wide)

(6) ㄺ → l   외곬 woegol (single-minded)

(7) ㄾ → l   핥다 halta (to lick)

(8) ㄿ → p   읊다 uip (to recite a poem)

(9) ㅄ → p   값 gap (price)

Supplementary Examples

달나라   dallara (moon)

동의보감   *Donguibogam*

    (The title of the Korean medical encyclopedia by *Heo Jun* published in 1614)

밖   bak (outside)

벗꽃   beotkkot (cherry blossom)

희망   huimang (hope)

The word order in Korean is

SUBJECT - Subject particle - VERB or Subject - object - object particle - verb.

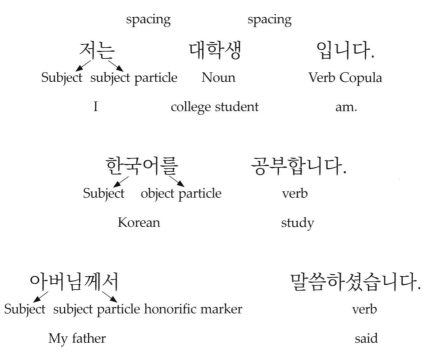

spacing   spacing

저는   대학생   입니다.

Subject subject particle   Noun   Verb Copula

I   college student   am.

한국어를   공부합니다.

Subject   object particle   verb

Korean   study

아버님께서   말씀하셨습니다.

Subject subject particle honorific marker   verb

My father   said

Spacing rules in Korean are according to Article 41 to Article 55 of the "Korean Spelling and Spacing Rules" which have been promulgated by the Ministry of Culture and Education and published by the National Institute of the Korean Language of the Republic of Korea. Here is a list of selected major points in spacing rules.

1. A space between an adjective and a noun
   아름다운 장미   a beautiful rose

2. A space between an adverb and a verb
   조용히 먹어요.   He/she is eating quietly

3. No spacing when a noun is followed by a copula.
   꽃입니다   It is a flower.

4. A space after a subject or object particle.
   A noun + subject particle or object particle and a verb
   교과서가 있습니다.   There is a textbook.
   컴퓨터를 삽니다.   I am buying a computer.

5. A space between a noun and another noun
   자가 격리   self-quarantine
   사회적 거리 두기   social distance

6. No spacing in proper nouns
   국립국어원   National Institute of the Korean Language

7. There is no space between a given name and the surnames, however, there is a space between a person's full name and any title
   김사량   Kim Sa-ryang
   김주영 씨   Mr. Ju-yong Kim
   최동식 박사   Dr. Choe Chi-won
   충무공 이순신 장군   Admiral Chungmugong Yi Sun-sin

제1과

인 사

Greetings

❖ 1. 인 사

A 안녕하세요?
How are you?

B 안녕하세요?
How are you?

A 처음 뵙겠습니다.
It is nice to meet you.

이토 신지입니다.
I am Ito Shinji.

교환 학생입니다.
I am an exchange student.

B 저는 김세리입니다.
I am Kim Seri.

만나서 반갑습니다.
I am glad to meet you.

A 안녕히 가세요.
Good-bye(to the person leaving)

B 안녕히 계세요.
Good-bye(to the person staying)

단어 Vocabulary

인사	Greetings
안녕하세요?	안녕하다 is the dictionary form ㅡ세요 is an injunctive verb ending 안녕하세요 is the generic greeting phrase regardless of time.
처음	for the first time
뵙겠습니다.	뵙다 is the dictionary form 뵙겠습니다. Verb stem 뵙+ future infix 겠+ Polite formal verb ending 습니다.
이토 신지	Ito Shinji – a name of a person
저	humble form for one's self
교환 학생	exchange student
김세리	Kim Se-ri, Surname and given name of a person
만나서	만나다 to meet 만나서 Verb stem 만나+ ending indication causation–어/아 서
만나서 반갑습니다.	I am pleased to meet you.
반갑습니다.	반갑습니다 Verb stem 반갑+ formal polite statement ending ㅂ/습니다

문법 Grammar

1   안녕하세요. Greeting expression which can be used at anytime of the day. The English equivalents are: "How are you," "Good morning," "Good afternoon," and "Good evening."

> 안녕히 가세요. "Good-bye" to the person leaving literally means "please go in peace."
> 안녕히 계세요. "Good-bye" to the person staying literally means "please stay in peace."

2   뵙겠습니다 comes from 뵙다 which is a humble form of "to see." 처음 뵙겠습니다 is a phrase for greeting a person for the first time.

> 뵙다   Dictionary form or verb stem
> 뵙겠다 Preserve the verb stem 뵙 + future infix 겠
> 뵙겠습니다. Verb stem 뵙 + future infix 겠 +
>   formal polite verb ending 습니다.

3   Noun + 이다 is a form is called the copula which means "to be."

> 입니다.   Statement
>   이토 신지입니다. I am Ito Shinji.
> 입니까?   Question form (Interrogative form)
>   대학생입니까? Are you a college student?

Dictionary form/ Verb stem	이다	반갑다
Statement	입니다.	반갑습니다.
Interrogative	입니까?	반갑습니까?

▌연습 Practice

1. I am Yuri. 유리입니다.
2. I am a student. 학생입니다.
3. I am Korean. 한국 사람입니다.
4. Nice to meet you. 처음 뵙겠습니다.
5. I am pleased to meet you. 반갑습니다.
6. Yurika is Japanese. 유리카는 일본 사람입니다.
7. Ray is American. 레이는 미국 사람입니다.
8. I am Lisa. 리사입니다.
9. I am a college student. 대학생입니다.
10. I am an exchange student. 교환 학생입니다.

▌응용 Utilization: How would you respond?

1. You met your Korean instructor at the university bookstore. How would you greet him/her.
   안녕하세요. 교수님.
   Note: Nouns in Korean do not have gender. Addressing your instructor or your boss at work by first names would be inappropriate.

2. Greet a person who you meet for the first time.
   처음 뵙겠습니다. 만나서 반갑습니다.

3. You are leaving the classroom after the class. The instructor is still in the classroom. Say good-bye to your instructor.
   안녕히 계세요. 교수님.

4. After having a cup of coffee with your colleague at work, both of you are leaving the place.
   안녕히 가세요.

5. You happen to run into Mr. Smith who is taking the Korean class. How would you greet him?

스미스씨, 안녕하세요?

▌읽기 Reading

Pure Korean words are nouns that cannot be converted into Chinese characters.

아이 child   벚꽃 cherry blossom   틀 frame

There are Korean words that can be converted to Chinese letters.

교과서 textbook   教科書   약속 appointment, promise   約束

Loan words are words from foreign languages

골프 golf   레몬 lemon   컴퓨터 computer   인스타그램 instagram   카메라 camera
테니스 tennis   페이스 북 Facebook   호텔 hotels   트럭 trucks   아이스크림 ice cream

제2과 🖊

한국어 교과서입니다.

The Korean Language Textbook

❖ 2. 한국어 교과서입니다.

A 이것이 무엇입니까?
What is this?

B 책입니다.
This is a book.

한국어 교과서입니다.
This is a Korean language textbook.

A 저것은 무슨 책입니까?
What kind of a book is that over there?

B 책이 아닙니다.
It is not a book.

케이팝 잡지입니다.
It is a K-Pop magazine.

▌단어 Vocabulary

이것	this
이	subject particle
무엇입니까?	What is this?
책입니다.	This is a book.
한국어 교과서입니다.	This is a Korean language textbook.
저것은 무슨 책입니까?	What kind of a book is that over there?
책이 아닙니다.	It is not a book.
케이팝 가수입니다.	He/She is a K-pop singer.
잡지입니다.	It is a K-Pop magazine.

문법 Grammar

1 Sentence structure

Subject - Subject particle - Verb ending

2 이것 this 그것 that 저것 that over there
여기 here 거기 there 저기 over there

	Objects	Places
This	이것	여기
That	그것	거기
That over there	저것	저기
What/Where	무엇	어디
Anything/ Anywhere	아무것	아무 데

피곤해서 <u>아무 데</u>도 가고 싶지 않아요.

I do not want to go anywhere since I am tired.

3 은/는 is a subject particle.
이/가 is a topic particle or marker.

오늘<u>은</u>   날씨<u>가</u>   좋아요.
  ↓   ↓
subject particle   topic particle
The weather today is nice.

This sentence contains two subjects. One subject is "today" and the another is the weather. Since the topic of the sentence is "the weather" a topic particle이/가 is used. For the main subject which is 오늘 meaning today, subject particles 은/는 will be used.

Subject vocabulary ending with a vowel 은
Subject vocabulary ending with a consonant 는
A vocabulary of topic ending with a vowel 가
A vocabulary of topic ending with a consonant 이

내일은 비가 와요. It will rain tomorrow.
보람은 시력이 좋아요. Boram has good eyesight.

4 About the verbs - There are briefly four types of verbs
  1. Action verbs   가다   오다   먹다   자다   읽다 듣다
  2. Descriptive verbs 바쁘다 예쁘다 좋다 나쁘다 크다 작다
  3. Copula   이다 to be   아니다 not to be
  4 Status verb   있다 to exist   없다 not exist

Among the four types of verbs, 이다 "to be" (I am, you are, he/she is) /아
니다 "not to be" (I am not, you are not, he/she is not) are verbs called "the
copula." The copula verbs are followed by a noun which functions as a
predicate.

Noun + 이다
  책입니다.   This is a book.
  교과서입니다.   This is a textbook.
  가수입니다.   I am a singer.
  의사입니다.   I am a doctor.

5 Interrogative copula verb ending
  When asking copula questions, preserve the verb stem and add ㅂ니까?
  이다   To be
  입니다   Declarative verb ending
  입니까?   Interrogative verb ending

6 Subject particles 은/는

The subject particle 은/는marks off the subject of the sentence. It can also be used when emphasizing the subject. When there are two subjects in one sentence, 이/가 functions as a topic subject particles which complement narrower topics.

이것은 교통 카드입니다.	This is a train or bus fare card.
	교통 카드 literally means "traffic card".
여기는 1층입니다.	This (here) is the first floor.
저것은 볼펜입니다.	That over there is a ballpoint pen.

Example

이 백화점은 물건 값이 비쌉니다.	The prices in this department store is high.
유나는 한국 사람이 아닙니다.	Yuna is not Korean.
서울은 교통이 복잡합니다.	The traffic is congested in Seoul.
저는 키가 커요.	I am tall.
리나는 대학교 일학년이 됩니다.	Rina becomes a freshman college student.

▌연습 Practice

1. This is a book.   이것은 책입니다.
2. Is this a textbook?   이것은 교과서입니까?
3. This is not a magazine.   그것은 잡지가 아닙니다.
4. This is my father.   아버지입니다.
5. Is this my mother.   어머니입니까?
6. Are you a family?   가족입니까?
7. He/She is a professor.   교수님입니다.
8. He/She is a honor student.   우등생입니다.
9. This is a third grader textbook.   이것은 삼 학년 교과서입니다.
10. Those are chopsticks.   그것은 젓가락입니다.

응용 Utilization

1. You found an object which looks like a Korean traditional pouch. Ask your friend what it is. Your friend says it is a traditional Korean pouch which brings luck.
   Friend: 이것이 무엇입니까?　You: 복 주머니입니다.

2. Ask your friend whether the book over there is a dictionary.
   저것은 사전입니까?

3. You are pointing at what looks like an i-phone charger.
   이것은 충전기입니까?

4. Say to your friend that the thing near him/her is not a book.
   이것은 책이 아닙니다.

5. The thing your friend is holding is a magazine.
   그것은 잡지입니다.

Verb Stem · Dictionary Form	ㅂ니다/ 습니다.	ㅂ니까?/습니까?
이다 to be I am you are he/she is	입니다.	입니까?
아니다 to not to be I am not, you are not, he/she is not	아닙니다	아닙니까?
있다 to exist There is/ there are	있습니다.	있습니까?
없다 to not exist There is not/are not	없습니다.	없습니까?

여기가 어디입니까?

Around Seoul

❖ 3. 여기가 어디입니까?

A 여기가 어디입니까?
Where is this place?

B 경복궁입니다.
Here is *Gyungbok* Palace.

경복궁은 서울에 있습니다.
Gyungbok Palace is in Seoul.

A 여기는요?
What about here?

B 한옥 마을입니다.
It is a *Hanok* Korean traditional village.

A 정말 아름답습니다.
It is truly beautiful.

B 네. 서울에는 유네스코 문화 유산이 많이 있습니다.
Yes. There are many UNESCO designated cultural heritage sites in Seoul.

▌ 단어 Vocabulary

여기	here 가 is a subject particle especially indicating a specific topic.
어디	where
경복궁	*Gyungbok* Palace
서울	Seoul, the capital of Republic of Korea (South Korea)
여기는요?	What about here ?
한옥 마을	*Hanok* Korean traditional village
정말	truly
아름답습니다	It is beautiful.
유네스코 문화 유산	UNESCO designated cultural heritage

문법 Grammar

1 경복궁은 서울에 있습니다. *Gyungbok* Palace is in Seoul

이다 "to be" dictionary form	있다 "to exist"
입니다. This is/That is ….	있습니다 There is/There are
입니까? Is this/ Is that…?.	있습니까? Is there…/Are there …?.

Copula

Noun + 이다

Noun + subject particle 이/가 + 아니다

> 이것은 한국어 교과서입니다.
> This is a Korean textbook.
> 이것은 중국어 교과서가 아닙니다.
> This is not a Chinese textbook.

있다/ 없다

자동차가 있습니다. There is a car.
자리가 없습니다. There are no seats.

Process showing how verb endings are formed:
First, preserve the verb stem or verb root, and then apply the endings.

있다	아름답다
있습니다. There is/ there are	아름답습니다. It is beautiful.
있습니까? Is there?/ are there?	아름답습니까? Is it beautiful?

Action verb	오다 to come	오 + ㅂ니다 → 옵니다. 오 + ㅂ니까? → 옵니까?
	하다 to do	하 + ㅂ니다 → 합니다. 하 + ㅂ니까? → 합니까?
	읽다 to read	읽 + 습니다. → 읽습니다. 읽 + 습니까? → 읽습니까?
Descriptive verb	바쁘다	바쁘 + ㅂ니다 → 바쁩니다. 바쁘 +ㅂ니까? → 바쁩니까?
	아름답다 to be busy	아름답 + 습니다. → 아름답습니다. 아름답 + 습니까? → 아름답습니까?

2. 에 location particle
경복궁은 서울에 있습니다.
Gyungbok Palace is in Seoul.

3. Noun+ 은/는요 When the speaker is indicating the same topic mentioned in the previous sentence, instead of saying the entire sentence, the subject and the subject particle 은/는 is used assuming the given information.

4. 아름답다 Descriptive verb "to be beautiful"
-ㅂ니다. - 습니다.   Formal polite verb ending

Verb stems with *batchim* - add the suffix 습니다
    먹다 - 먹습니다
Verb stems without *batchim*
    바쁘다- 바쁩니다.

Irregular patterns 만들다 - *Batchim*ㄹ is dropped and ㅂ니다 is replaced.

Action verbs

Verb stem in ending vowel + ㅂ니다

가다 to go 가+ㅂ니다-갑니다.

Verb stem ending in consonant + 습니다.

찾다 to look for 찾+습니다 - 찾습니다.

Descriptive verbs

Verb stem ending in vowel + ㅂ니다

Verb stem ending in consonant + -습니다.

바쁘다 - 바쁘 + ㅂ니다 - 바쁩니다.

아름답다 - 아름답 + 습니다 - 아름답습니다.

ㄹ Irregular verbs

Verb stem ㄹ is drop ped and ㅂ니다 is added.

만들다 - 만듭니다.

길다 - 깁니다.

Copula: Noun + 이다

1. 서울입니다.　It is Seoul.
2. 경복궁입니다.　It is *Gyungbok* Palace.
3. 박물관입니다.　It is a museum.
4. 미술관입니다.　It is a gallery.
5. 주차장입니다.　It is a parking lot.

Action verb stem + ㅂ/습니까?

Action verb stem + ㅂ/습니다.

1. 가다 to go
   자전거로 갑니까? → 네. 자전거로 옵니다.
   Are you going by bicycles?

2. 오다 to come
   학교에 옵니까? → 네. 학교에 옵니다.
   Are you coming to school?

3. 쓰다 to write
   책을 씁니까? → 책을 씁니다.
   Are you writing a book?

4. 읽다 to read
   시를 읽습니까? → 시를 읽습니다.
   Are you reading a poem?

5. 말하다 to speak/to say
   일어로 말합니까? → 일어로 말합니다.
   Are you speaking in Japanese?

Descriptive verb stem + ㅂ/습니까?
Descriptive verb stem + ㅂ/습니다.

1. 바쁘다 to be busy   바쁩니까? → 바쁩니다.
2. 예쁘다 to be pretty   예쁩니까? → 예쁩니다.
3. 많다   to be many   많습니까? → 많습니다.
4. 멀다   to be far   멉니까? → 멉니다.
5. 가깝다 to be close   가깝습니까? → 가깝습니다.

To exist/ to not exist 있다/없다

1. 꽃이 많이 있습니까?   Are there are a lot of flowers?
   네. 꽃이 많이 있습니다.
   아니요. 꽃이 많이 없습니다.
2. 영수증이 있습니까?   Do you have a receipt?
   네. 영수증이 있습니다.
   아니요. 영수증이 없습니다.
3. 자전거는 있습니까?   Are there any bicycles?
   네. 자전거가 있습니다.
   아니요. 자전거가 없습니다.
4. 열쇠가 있습니까?   Is there a key?
   네. 열쇠가 있습니다.
   아니요. 열쇠가 없습니다.
5. 컴퓨터가 있습니까?.   Are there computers?
   네. 컴퓨터가 있습니다.
   아니요. 컴퓨터가 없습니다.

응용 Utilization-Question and Answer

1. Are you going? 갑니까? → 네. 갑니다.

2. Are you buying? 삽니까? → 네. 삽니다.

3. Are you waiting? 기다립니까? → 네. 기다립니다.

4. Is he sleeping? 주무십니까? → 네. 주무십니다.

5. Where is *Gyungbok* Palace? 경복궁은 어디에 있습니까?
   Gyungbok Palace is located in Seoul. 경복궁은 서울에 있습니다.

6. Is the *Han River* in Seoul?
   한강은 서울에 있습니까? → 네. 서울에 있습니다.

7. This place is beautiful. 아름답습니다.

8. You do not know the name of the place you are now at.
   여기가 어디입니까?

9. This is a listed UNESCO World Heritage site.
   여기는 유네스코 세계문화유산지입니다.

10. This is a park. 공원입니다.

11. These are flowers. 꽃입니다.

12. Yuka is a writer. 유카는 작가입니다.

13. Ming Ming is Chinese. 밍밍은 중국 사람입니다.

14. Van is Vietnamese. 밴은 월남/베트남 사람입니다.

▌읽기 Reading

Names of places in Seoul

| 남대문 | 시청 | 광화문 | 덕수궁 | 창경궁 | 서울타워 |

제 4 과

가족 사진

Family Photograph

❖ 4. 가족 사진

A 이것 사진입니까?

Is this a photograph?

B 네, 옛날 가족 사진입니다.

Yes, it is an old family photograph.

A 여기 이 분은 누구입니까?

Who is this person here?

B 어머니입니다.

She is my mother.

어머니는 한국 전통 공예 선생님입니다.

My mother is a Korean craft artist.

제 가족은 아버지와 어머니, 형과 여동생입니다.

There are four members in my family: Father, mother, older brother, and younger sister.

형은 회사원입니다.

My older brother is a salaried employee.

A 남동생도 대학생입니까?

Is your younger brother also a college student?

B 아니요. 대학생이 아닙니다.

No. He is not a college student.

고등학생입니다.

He is a high school student.

단어 Vocabulary

이것	이것 this 이것 this 그것 that 저것 a thing over there
사진	photograph
네	"yes"
옛날	literally means "long ago"
옛날 가족사진	old family photograph taken long ago
입니다	Copula "to be" 이다 + formal polite ending ㅂ니다 – 입니다. 이다 to be 입니다 이 + ㅂ니다 formal polite ending
여기	여기 here 거기there 저기 over there away from the speaker and the listener
이 분	this person 분 is a honorific classifier for people
누구	who
어머니	mother
한국 전통 공예	Korean traditional handcraft
선생님	선생 means a teacher -님 is a generic honorific suffix for addressing a teacher or a person older than your self 아버님 addressing either one's own or a person's father 어머님 addressing either one's own or a person's mother 의사 선생님 doctor 교수님 professor 사장님 president of a company

제	"my" 저 is a humble form for referring to yourself 제 is a possessive humble pronoun 나 is a generic form for the first person singular
가족	family
Noun + 와/과	"and" a connective particle
아버지	father
어머니	mother
형	a male self addressing an older brother
여동생	younger sister
회사원	company employee
남동생	younger brother
도	a particle meaning also
대학생	college student

아니요.	"No"
	 아니다 to not be
	 아니요
	   아니 verb stem + informal polite ending 요
	 아닙니다
	   아니 verb stem + formal polite ㅂ니다

고등학생	high school student.

▌문법 Grammar

1. 분 is a honorific classifier for a person
   사람 is a general classifier for a person

   이 분은 누구세요?　Who is this person?
   그 분은 선생님입니까?　Is that person a teacher?
   저 분은 회장님입니다. That person is chairman (of a company).

2 Noun와/과 "and"
If a noun ends with a vowel 와
If a noun ends with a consonant 과

아버지와 어머니 Father and mother
형과 여동생 A male-self referring to an older brother and younger sister
오빠와 언니 A female-self referring to an older brother and older sister

3 Noun + 도 "also"
남동생도 대학생입니까?
    Is your brother also a college student
여기도 서울입니까?
    Is this place also Seoul?
오늘도 바쁩니다.
    I am also busy today.

4 Noun + 이다 (to be) — Noun + Subject Particle 아니다 (not to be)
Noun입니까? — Noun입니다
Noun (subject) + subject particle이 + 아닙니까? - Noun + 이 아닙니다.

이것 사진입니까? — 아니요. 사진이 아닙니다.
    Is this a photograph? — No. It is not.
가족입니까? — 아니요. 가족이 아닙니다.
    Are they your family members? — No. They are not.
중학생입니까? — 아니요. 중학생이 아닙니다.
    Are you a junior high school student? — No. I am not.

1 **Classifier for a person**

    1. 이 분은 소설가입니다.

       This person (honorific classifier) is a writer.

    2. 그 분은 어머니입니다.

       That person (honorific classifier) is not an accountant.

    3. 저 분은 의사 선생님입니다.

       The person over there is a doctor.

    4. 그 분은 누구세요?

       Who is that person? (honorific classifier)

    5. 일본 분입니까?

       Are you Japanese (honorific classifier)?

2 **Noun 와/과 "and"**

    1. 형과 남동생입니다.

       This is my older brother and my younger brother.

    2. 오빠와 여동생입니다. (The speaker is a female self.)

       This is my older brother and my younger sister.

    3. 할아버지와 할머니입니다.

       This is my grandfather and my grandmother

    4. 아버지와 언니입니다. (The speaker is a female self.)

       This is my father and my older sister.

    5. 누나와 형입니다. (The speaker is a male self)

       This is my older sister and my older brother.

3 **Noun + 도 "also"**

    1. 방탄소년단과 레드벨벳입니까?

       Are they BTS and Red Velvet?

    2. 이것도 세븐틴 사진입니까?

       Is this also a photograph of *Seventeen*.

    3. 이 분도 미국 사람입니다.

       This person is also an American.

4. 남동생도 회사원입니다.

   My younger brother is also a company employee.

5. 저도 한국 사람입니다.

   I am also Korean.

4 Noun + 이다/아니다"

1. 화장품입니까?　　Is this a cosmetic?

   네. 화장품입니다.　　Yes, it is a cosmetic.

   아니요. 화장품이 아닙니다.　No, it is not a cosmetic.

2. 일본 사람입니까? Are you Japanese?

   네. 일본 사람입니다. Yes, I am Japanese.

   아니요. 일본 사람이 아닙니다. I am not Japanese.

3. 유학생입니까?　　Are you a student from overseas?

   네. 유학생입니다.　　Yes, I am a student from overseas.

   아니요. 유학생이 아닙니다. No, I am not a student from overseas.

4. 점심 시간입니까? Is it lunch time?

   네. 점심 시간입니다. Yes, it is lunch time.

   아니요. 점심 시간이 아닙니다. No, it is not lunch time.

5. 오늘 휴일입니까?　Is today a holiday?

   네. 휴일입니다.　Yes, today is a holiday.

   아니요. 휴일이 아닙니다.　No, today is not a holiday.

응용 Utilization

1. Asking someone whether today is a holiday.
   오늘 휴일입니까?

2. Asking your friend whether the person here is his father.
   이 분이 아버지/아버님입니까?

3. Is your younger sister in highschool?
   여동생이 고등학생입니까?

4. Your older brother is a company employee.
   If the self is a man 형이 회사원입니까?
   If the speaker is a woman 오빠가 회사원입니까?

5. Introduce your family. (Sample phrases)
   안녕하세요.

   제 가족을 소개합니다.

   제 가족은 아버지와 어머니, 형과 누나, 남동생과 여동생입니다.

   아버지는 회사원입니다.

   어머니는 독서지도사입니다.

   형은 대학원생입니다.

   누나는 프로그래머입니다.

   남동생과 여동생은 고등학생입니다.

   귀여운 강아지 바둑이도 우리 가족입니다.

도서관은 어디에 있습니까?

Location

❖ 5. 도서관은 어디에 있습니까?

A   도서관은 어디에 있습니까?
Where is the library?

B   구글 지도에는 여기입니다.
Google Maps says it is here.

A   어느 쪽에 있습니까?
Which way is it?

B   학생 회관 옆에 있습니다.
It is at the side of the Student Center.

A   저 건물 안에 무엇이 있습니까?
What is inside that building?

B   서점과 편의점이 있습니다.
There is a bookstore and a convenience store.

단어 Vocabulary

도서관	library
어디	where
에	location particle
있습니까?	Is there?/Are there? 있다 to exist 있습니까? Interrogative question form of 있다
구글	Google
지도	map
여기	here
어느 쪽	which direction
학생 회관	Student Center
옆	side
저	"that over there"
건물	building
안	inside
무엇	what
서점	bookstore
편의점	convenience store

문법 Grammar

1 Location + 에는 is an particle emphasizing a location as a topic

회의장 앞에는 사무실이 있습니다.

In front of the conference hall, there <u>is</u> an office.

경주에는 왕릉과 고분이 있습니다.

In *Gyeongju* city, there <u>are</u> royal tombs and ancient tombs.

가방 안에는 무엇이 있습니까?

What <u>is</u> inside the briefcase?

2 Formal polite endings:

Statement	Verb stem + ㅂ니다/습니다
Interrogative	Verb stem + ㅂ니다/ 습니까?

있다/ 없다   to exist/ to not exist

있다 to exist   없다   to not exist

있습니다 There is/There are   없습니다. There is not/ There are no

있습니까? Is there…/Are there …. 없습니까? Is there not/ Are there not

연극박물관이 어디에 있습니까?

Where is the Theater Museum?

무라카미 하루키 뮤지엄은 옆 건물입니다.

Next to the building, there is the Murakami Haruki Museum.

꽃집 앞에 문구점이 있습니다.

There is a stationery store in front of the flower shop.

연습 Practice

1. 구글 지도에는 없습니다.   It is not in Google Maps.
2. 운동장 안에는 있습니다.   It is inside the playground.
3. 박물관에는 책이 있습니까?   Are there books in the museum?
4. 학교에는 편의점이 있습니다. At school, there are convenience stores.
5. 앞에는 건물이 없습니까?   Is there a building in front (this place)?
6. 문구점이 있습니까?   Is there a stationary store?
7. 은행 뒤에는 카페가 있습니다. There is a café at the back of the bank.
8. 화장실은 건물 옆에 있습니다.   There is a rest room next to the building.
9. 학생 회관 왼쪽에 있습니다.   It is on the left side of the Student Center.
10. 오른쪽에 피자 집이 있습니다. On the right side, there is a pizza place.

응용 Utilization

1. It is in front of the dormitory.
   기숙사 앞에 있습니다.
2. The movie theater is on the righthand side.
   영화관 오른쪽에 있습니다.
3. The toilet is on the lefthand side.
   화장실은 왼쪽에 있습니다.
4. The classroom is behind the office.
   교실은 사무실 뒤에 있습니다.
5. Embassy of Japan is at Insadong.
   일본 대사관은 인사동에 있습니다.
6. The Consulate of the United States is in Nagoya.
   미국 영사관은 나고야에 있습니다.
7. Are there play grounds inside the park?
   공원 안에 놀이터가 있습니까?
8. Inside the drawer, there is an eraser.
   서랍 안에 지우개가 있습니다.

9. To the righthand side, there is an auditorium.
   오른쪽에 강당이 있습니다.

10. There are no ATMs (automated teller machines).
    현금입출기는 없습니다.

제6과

어떻게 지내십니까?

Daily Greetings

❖ 6. 어떻게 지내십니까?

A 오래간만입니다.
I have not seen you for a long time.

요즘 어떻게 지내십니까?
How have you been?

B 잘 지냅니다.
I am fine.

한국말 배우느라 바쁩니다.
I am busy because I am learning Korean.

A 점심은 학교에서 먹습니까?
Do you have lunch at school?

B 네. 학교 식당에서 먹습니다.
Yes, I eat at the cafeteria.

A 집에는 지하철로 가십니까?
Do you go home by subway?

B 네. 지하철로 갑니다.
Yes, I take subway.

▌단어 Vocabulary

오래간만	"for a long time" 오래간만입니다 is a greeting expression used to a person who you have already met or know. The idiomatic greeting means "I have not seen you in a long time. Good to see you."
어떻게	how

지내십니까?	Comes from the verb 지내다 meaning "to spend time" and the ending contains a formal polite inquisitive/question form.
	지내다 to spend time
	지내시다 Verb stem 지내 + honorific infix 시
	지내십니까?
	  Verb stem 지내 + honorific infix 시 + formal polite inquisitive ㅂ니까?
	잘 지냅니다. "I am very well or I am fine."
	  잘 is an adverb meaning "very"

한국말	the Korean language
배우느라	"because I am learning" 배우다 to learn 배우느라 Verb stem 배우 + causation connective 느라
바쁩니다.	"I am busy." 바쁘다 to be busy 바쁩니다. Verb stem 바쁘 + formal polite ending ㅂ니다.

63

점심	lunch
학교에서	at school
먹습니까?	"Do you eat?" 먹다 to eat 먹습니까? Verb stem 먹다 + formal polite inquisitive ending 습니까?
학교 식당	school cafeteria
에서	location particle "at"
집	home
지하철	subway
로	by

가십니까?	"Do you go ···"
	가다 to go
	가시다 Verb stem가 + honorific infix시
	가십니까?
	  Verb stem가+ honorific infix시 + ㅂ니까? formal
	  polite inquisitive ending

문법 Grammar

1. Verb stem + (으)시 is an honorific infix. When asking a question to a person or referring to another person, an honorific infix is included. An honorific infix is not used when addressing the self.

지내다 - 지내<u>시</u>다
오다 - 오<u>시</u>다
가다 - 가<u>시</u>다

Irregular honorific conjugations

먹다 to eat – 잡수시다 드시다
자다 to go to bed – 주무시다
있다 a person exists – 계시다

Regular honorific –시–

지내십니까? How are you?
지내시다   Verb stem 지내 + honorific infix 시
지내십니까? Verb stem 지내 + honorific infix 시 +
          formal polite inquisitive ㅂ니까?

There are also honorific nouns such as 진지 for referring to a meal, 연세 for age, and 존함 for names. A comparison between a plain form without honorific nouns and with honorific nouns.

Plain	Honorific	
밥을 먹습니다.	진지 meal	진지를 드십니다.
나이가 칠십입니다	연세 age	연세가 칠십이십니다.
이름이 홍길동입니다.	존함 name	존함이 홍길동이십니다.

2 Verb stem + 느라 is a connective ending stating a causation for the second clause.

한국말 배우느라 바쁩니다.

I am busy because I am learning Korean.

운동하느라 바쁩니다.

I am busy because I am working out.

레포트를 쓰느라 시간이 없습니다.

I do not have time because I am writing a term paper.

3 Noun + 에서 "at"

에서 is a location particle used in conjunction with either nouns or verbs to mark the location of an action. If an action has beginning and ending, such as 공부하다 "to study," or "to eat," a location particle indicating where an act of studying begins and ends, 에서 is used.

도서관에서 공부합니다.   I study at the library.

학교 식당에서 먹습니다.   I eat at the cafeteria.

백화점에서 쇼핑합니다.   I shop at the department store.

There is another location particle 에 ("to") denoting a particular place or destination. In a sentence, 도서관에 갑니다. "I am going to the library," or 학교 식당에 갑니다. "I am going to the cafeteria" 에 is a location particle indicating a library or a cafeteria as a particular place of destination.

4 먹습니까? comes from 먹다 to eat + 습니까? formal polite question form
Verb stem + ㅂ/습니다 is for a formal polite statement ending

> **Action verb stem + formal polite inquisitive ending ㅂ/습니까?**
> **Action verb stem + formal polite statement ending ㅂ/습니다.**

먹습니까? Are you eating? — 먹습니다. I am eating.
가십니까? Are you going? (Honorific infix 시) — 갑니다. I am going.
만납니까? Are you meeting someone? — 만납니다. I am meeting someone.

> **Descriptive verb stem + formal polite inquisitive ending ㅂ/습니까?**
> **Descriptive verb stem + formal polite statement ending ㅂ/습니다.**

어렵습니까? Is it difficult? — 어렵습니다. It is difficult.
교실이 넓습니까? Is the classroom spacious? —
　　교실이 넓습니다. It is spacious.
바쁘십니까? Are you busy (Honorific infix 시) — 바쁩니다. I am busy.

5　Noun + (으)로 means "by means of"

자동차로 갑니다.　I go by car.
지하철로 갑니다.　I go by subway.
버스로 갑니다.　　I go by bus.

연습 Practice

Action verbs with the honorific infix

1. 가십니까? Are you going? — 네. 갑니다. Yes, I am going.
2. 오십니까? Are you coming? — 네. 옵니다. Yes, I am coming.
3. 선생님께서 바쁘십니까? (To the instructor) Are you busy?
　네. 바쁩니다. Yes, I am busy.

4. 진지를 드십니까? Are you having a meal?

네. 먹습니다. Yes, I am having a meal.

5. 읽으십니까? Are you reading?

네. 읽습니다. Yes, I am reading.

Descriptive verbs

1. 기쁩니까? Are you delighted? — 기쁩니다. I am delighted.

2. 비쌉니까? Is it expensive? — 비쌉니다. It is expensive.

3. 슬픕니까? Are you sad? — 슬픕니다. I am sad.

4. 아름답습니까? Is it beautiful? — 아름답습니다. It is beautiful.

5. 어렵습니까? Is it difficult? — 어렵습니다. It is difficult.

Verb stem + (으)느라

1. 자느라 정거장을 놓쳤습니다.

I missed the bus stop because I was sleeping.

2. 이사하느라 힘듭니다.

I am having a hard time due to moving.

3. 신문을 읽느라 아침을 못 먹습니다.

Since I am reading the newspaper, I cannot have breakfast.

4. 인터넷을 검색하느라 전화를 못 받습니다.

Since I am surfing the Internet, I cannot answer the phone calls.

5. 뉴스를 보느라 바쁩니다.

I am busy because I am watching the news.

Location + 에서

1. 카페에서 카푸치노를 마십니다.

I am having a cup of cappuccino.

2. 연필을 문구점에서 삽니다.

I buy pencils at the stationery store.

3. 설악산에서 도시락을 먹습니다.

I am having lunch (eating from the lunch box) at Mt. Seolak.

4. 사무실에서 팩스를 보냅니다.

I am sending a fax from the office.

5. 공원에서 산책을 합니다.

   I am going for a walk in the park.

Noun + (으)로 "by means of"

1. 자전거로 갑니다. I go by bicycle.
2. 버스로 갑니다. I go by bus.
3. 전철로 갑니다. I go by train.
4. 자동차로 갑니다. I go by car.
5. 지하철로 갑니다. I go by subway.

응용 Utilization

1. Greet and ask your former boss who you have not seen for a while.
   오래간만입니다. 어떻게 지내셨습니까?

2. Say to your friend you are busy learning Korean.
   한국말 배우느라 바쁩니다.

3. You eat dinner at home.
   저녁은 집에서 먹습니다.

4. Ask your friend's father where he eats lunch?
   점심은/진지는 어디에서 드십니까?

5. Say to your friends the book is expensive.
   책이 비쌉니다.

6. You commute by subway.
   지하철로 다닙니다.

7. Ask your boss where he/she is heading.
   어디 가십니까?

8. You do not have time because you are writing a term paper.
   레포트 쓰느라 시간이 없습니다.

9. Since I am studying, I have been busy
   공부하느라 바쁩니다.

10. You come to school by bicycle.
    자전거로 옵니다.

읽기 Reading

아버님께서는 샐러드와 샌드위치를 드십니다. 책도 읽으십니다.
저는 빵과 과일을 먹습니다.

In Korean verbs, three speech styles are usually used depending who you are having conversation with. Socio lingustic elements are added when a person greets in polite endings. Proper body language is also followed when greeting to one's superior or someone older than the speaker. In some cultures, a man raising his hat momentarily if he is wearing one will be a polite way of greeting someone. In Korean, slightly inclining the upper body when greeting would be desirable.

Formal polite ending   안녕하십니까?
Informal polite ending 안녕하세요?
Blunt form   안녕!

언제 졸업합니까?

Future Plans

❖ 7. 언제 졸업합니까?

A 언제 졸업합니까?
When are you graduating?

B 내년에 졸업합니다.
I will graduate next year.

A 졸업하면 뭐 하실 거예요?
What will you do when you graduate?

B 취직하고 싶습니다.
I would like to get a job.

단어 Vocabulary

언제	when
졸업합니까?	…are you graduating? 졸업하다 to graduate 졸업합니까? 　Verb stem 졸업하 + formal inquisitive ending ㅂ니까?
내년	next year
작년	last year
올해	this year
에	location, time particle
뭐	Contracted version of 무엇 "what"
을	object particle
하실 거예요.	…will probably … 하다　　　to do 하시다　　Verb stem 하 + honorific infix 시 하실 거예요. Verb stem 하 + honorific infix 시 + 　　　future tense informal polite ㄹ 거예요.
취직하고 싶어요	… want to be employeed 취직하다 to get employed 취직하고 싶다 　Verb stem 취직하+ending for "to want to"고 싶다. 취직하고 싶어요 　Verb stem 취직하+ ending for "to want to"고 싶다 　+informal polite ending 어요.

문법 Grammar

1 -에 can be used for both location and time particle

내년에 유학 가요.　I will leave for study abroad next year.

몇 시에 떠나요?　What time does it leave?

학교에 있어요.　I am at school.

2 Verb stem + (으)면　when, if

이것이 좋으면 사요.　If this is good, I will buy it.

돈이 있으면 투자하세요.　If you have some money, please invest in them.

한국 사람이면 사증은 필요없어요.

If you are a Korean, you do not need a visa.

3 Verb stem + (으)ㄹ 거예요?　and Verb stem + (으)ㄹ 것이에요?　are the terminative endings which denote supposition of an act or probable future, meaning "…will probably …"

이 서류를 번역할 거예요.　I will probably translate this document.

복사할 거예요.　I will probably make a copy.

박물관에 갈 거예요. I will probably go to the museum.

연습 Practice

에 as a time particle

1. I will participate in study abroad next year.　내년에 유학 가요.
2. I will go in the afternoon.　오후에 가겠습니다.
3. I will eat in the morning.　아침에 먹겠어요.
4. I get up at dawn.　새벽에 일어나요.
5. It usually snows at night.　주로 밤에 눈이 와요.

Verb stem + (으)면 when, if

1. 그 가구가 좋으면 삽시다. If that piece of furniture is good, let's buy it.
2. 돈이 있으면 투자하세요. If you have some money, please invest them.
3. 한국사람이면 사증은 필요없어요.
   If you are Korean, you do not need a visa.
4. 이가 아프면 치과에 가요. If you have a toothache, visit the dentist.
5. 방을 정리하면 깨끗해져요. If you organize your room, it will be clean.

Verb stem + (으) ㄹ 거예요? Verb stem + (으) ㄹ 것이에요?

1. 시험을 치실 거예요? Are you going to take the examination?
2. 유럽 여행하실 거예요? Are you going to travel in Europe?
3. 금강산에 가실 거예요? Will you be visiting Mt. Gumgang
4. 예쁜 옷을 입으실 거예요? Will you be wearing a pretty dress?
5. 도시에 사실 거예요? Will you live in a city?

Verb stem + 고 싶다.

1. 취직하고 싶어요. I would like to be employeed.
2. 패션디자이너가 되고 싶습니다. I would like to become a fashion designer.
3. 예쁜 옷을 입고 싶어요. I would like to wear a pretty dress.
4. 눈이 오면 밖으로 나가고 싶어요. When the snow comes, I would like to go out.
5. 큰집을 사고 싶어요. I would like to buy a big house.

응용 Utilization

1. Where are you going? 어디에 가요? 어디에 가세요? 어디에 가십니까?
2. It is on the Internet. 인터넷에 있어요.
3. I write in my pocket notebook. 수첩에 씁니다./ 수첩에 써요.
4. If you study, it would not be difficult. 공부하면 어렵지 않아요.
5. If you are on a business trip, please meet Mr. Smith.
   출장가면 스미스씨 만나세요.

6. If the traffic is congested, take a bus. 교통이 복잡하면 버스로 가요.
7. If I have time, I will go. 시간이 있으면 가겠어요.
8. If you are ill, go to an emergency room. 아프면 응급실로 가세요.
9. The instructor will probably eat *gimbap*. 선생님은 김밥을 드실 거예요.
10. You will probably get promoted. 승진할 거예요.

읽기 Reading

입학식과 졸업식

한국에서는 3월초에 초등학교, 중학교, 고등학교, 대학교에서 입학식이 있습니다. 입학식 날에는 보통 수업이 없습니다. 졸업식은 주로 2월에 있습니다. 코로나 때문에 작년에는 온라인 졸업식이 있었습니다.

날씨가 참 좋지요?

Weather

❖ 8. 날씨가 참 좋지요?

A   날씨가 참 좋지요?

It is very nice, isn't it?

B   네. 그렇군요.

Yes. I agree.

봄 날씨이네요.

It is indeed spring weather.

A   제 고향은 경상북도 경주입니다.

My hometown is Gyeongju in Gyeongsangbuk Province.

이런 날은 고향 생각이 나지요.

This kind of day makes me to think of my hometown.

봄에는 개나리와 진달래가 피지요.

In spring, forsythia and azalea bloom.

무궁화 꽃도 피네요.

Also, the national flower of Korea, *Mugunghwa* blooms.

단어 Vocabulary

날씨	weather
참	very
좋지요?	It is good, isn't it? 좋다 to be good 좋지요? 　Verb stem 좋+ending to seek an agreement 지요
그렇군요.	It is indeed so. 그렇다 to be so 그렇군요. 　Verb stem 그렇+ending for confiming 군요
봄	spring
여름	summer
가을	autumn
겨울	winter
제	my
고향	hometown
경상북도	*Gyeongsangbuk* Province
경주	*Gyeongju*
이런 날	this kind of day
생각	thought
개나리	forsythia 개나리 symbolizes the first flower to bloom in spring.
진달래	azealia
피지요	"it will certainly bloom." 피다 to bloom 피지요 　Verb stem 피+ terminative ending for seeking an agreement 지요

문법 Grammar

1 Verb stem + 지요? "I believe..." "I bet" "I guess..."

Verb stem + 지요 or Verb stem + 지요? is a suppositive ending which means "supposedly." It is a verb ending used when seeking the listener's agreement to, confirmation of or reassurance about the statement by the speaker. The ending is similar to tag questions in English expressed at the end of a sentence as "isn't it?" or "aren't they?" It is used either as a statement or in a question form.

부모님께서도 안녕하시지요?

I would assume your parent are fine, aren't they?

많이 아프지요?

It must hurting, doesn't it?

너무 비싸지요?

It must be very expensive, right?

창문이 너무 작지요?

This window is too small, isn't it.

2 Verb stem + (는) 군요 is an exclamatory verb ending expressing delight, sudden realization, surprise, or confirming the speaker's statement. "...is/are indeed.." "I see..." "so it is..."

미세먼지가 많군요. (Surely), there is a lot of ultra-fine industrial dust.

영화가 재미있군요. The movie seems to be interesting.

경치가 좋군요.   What a nice view!

그렇군요. (Confirming what the speaker said) Yes, it is

3 Verb stem + (이)네요.

Colloquial verb ending confirming a fact or the speaker's statement.

This lesson, in particular, introduces similar colloquial verb endings. We can infer from the verb endings that spoken Korean is "the other - oriented." When the speaker is not completely sure about what he/she is saying, or you are conscious about the listener, or the speaker wants to respect the listner's unknown opinion or something that is not yet said, endings such as Verb stem + 지요, Verb stem + 군요, and Verb stem + 네요 terminative endings imply politely seeking the listener's agreement. 오늘이 제 생일이네요. (I realize today is my birthday.) Verb stem + (이)네요 ending functions as affirming a fact or what the speaker said.

Noun + 이에요 is a plain declarative verb ending describing the status of an object or a situation. It is a straight forward statement that does not necessarily imply the listener's agreement or confirmation. In most cases, these three endings can be interchangeably used agreeing with the person's statement. These endings may be similar to hedging or tag expressions in English. Hedging phrases function to protect the speaker's claim. Hedging or tag phrases may sound vague or not as being uncertain. All three endings 지요, -군요, -네요 imply meanings such as "it may indicate," "could be said," "might," "may," or "could/would you agree with what I said?"

벌써 아홉 시 이네요.	I did not realize it is already nine o'clock.
여기는 절이네요.	I see, this place here is a temple.
내일부터 휴일이네요.	I now realize that from tomorrow it is a holiday.

연습 Practice

Verb stem + 지요

1. 한국에도 비가 많이 오지요. It rains a lot in Korea also, doesn't it?
2. 댁으로 돌아가시지요. I suggest that you return to your place.
3. 그분은 의사이시지요? I am sure he is a doctor, isn't he?
4. 이 자동차는 안전하지요? I would assume this car is safe.
5. 집에서 쉬어야지요. I suggest it is better for you to take a rest at home.

Verb stem + 군요

1. 동경은 날씨가 춥군요. I find the weather in Tokyo to be cold.
2. 드라마가 재미있군요. I find the drama very interesting.
3. 달이 밝군요. The moon is very bright.
4. 상냥하군요. You are kind and good-hearted.
5. 이 집은 참 아늑하군요. This house is very cozy.

Verb stem + 네요.

1. 벚꽃이 피네요. Cherry flowers are (surely) blooming.
2. 아직 바쁘네요. I am still busy.
3. 조금 비싸네요. I think it is a bit expensive.
4. 진달래가 아름답네요. Azalea is (indeed) beautiful.
5. 경치가 멋있네요. The view is magnificent.

응용 Utilization

1. I bet taking a subway train would be much faster than going by car.
   자동차보다는 지하철이 빠르겠지요?
2. I believe you will keep your promise.
   약속은 지키시겠지요.
3. I will, for sure, help you anytime
   언제든지 도와 드리지요.

4. The U.S. is, indeed, spacious.
   미국은 참 넓군요.

5. This movie is truly interesting. (Don't you agree with me?)
   이 영화는 정말 재미있군요.

6. Would you know by any chance when the chairman will come?
   회장님께서 언제 오시는지 알고 계시나요?

7. Would you kindly please tell me how to go?
   어떻게 가는지 말씀해 주실 수 있나요?

8. Would you know by any chance how to solve that problem?
   그 문제를 푸는 방법을 아시나요?

9. Do you think I can do well like Mika if I try hard?
   열심히 하면 미카처럼 잘 할 수 있나요?

10. Would you please send that document quickly?
    그 서류를 좀 빨리 보내줄 수 없나요?

▌읽기 Reading

봄날

벚꽃이 피나봐요.
이 겨울도 끝이 나요.
보고 싶다. 보고 싶다.

(방탄소년단의 노래 Kim, Yong-dae, BTS The Review 2020, p.176 Seoul RH KOREA)

무궁화 *Mugunghwa*

In the movie, *Squid Game* 오징어게임, a giant girl figure dressed in yellow and orange says, 무궁화 꽃이 피었습니다. *"Mugunghwa kkochi pieot seumnida"* which means "The Hibiscus Flowers Bloomed."

무궁화 꽃이 피었습니다

The Hibiscus Flowers Bloomed.

The group stands on one end of the playing area, at the starting line. The person who is "It" stands at the other end, at the finish line, usually facing a tree.

The person who's "It" stands with his back to the group. He/She says, 무궁화 꽃이 피었습니다 *(Mugunghwa kkochi pieot seumnida)*. Then he quickly turns around to face the group.

While he is facing away from the group, the people in the group run towards the finish line. Meanwhile, as soon as the one who is "It" finishes saying, *무궁화 꽃이 피었습니다* he/she will quickly turns around to face the group. The group must freeze. Anyone who is seen moving has to hold hands with the one who is "It". After the first person joins hands with the one who is "It", the other people caught moving join hands with the other people who were seen moving, forming a chain.

The game continues like this until someone reaches the finish line and touches the person who's "It". Then everyone runs away while the one who is "It" tries to catch them. In Japan, there is a similar play saying "*Ta-rumasan ga koronnda*" meaning "Taruma san fell over."

제9과

전공이 무엇이에요?

Majors in college

❖ 9. 전공이 무엇이에요?

A 전공이 무엇이에요?

What is your major?/ What are you majoring in?

B 국제관계학이에요.

I major in International Affairs.

진수 씨는요?

What about you, Jinsu?

A 저는 한국 문학이에요.

I am majoring in Korean Literature.

역사학에도 관심이 있어요.

I am also interested in history.

단어 Vocabulary

전공	major
무엇	what
국제관계학	study of international relations
진수	Jinsu (a person's first name) Name + 씨 polite marker for either a first or a family name of another
한국 문학	Korean literature
역사	history
에	in/at (particle)
도	also (particle)
관심이 있어요.	interested in …

문법 Grammar

1 Noun + ㄴ/는요?

When referring to a same prior theme to the same addressee, Noun + ㄴ/는요? meaning "what about in your case" is used.

제 전공은 언어학이에요. 타쿠 씨는요?
My major is linguistics. What about you, Taku?
저는 고전 문학이 좋아요. 진경 씨는요?
I like classical literature. What about you, Jinkyung?
제 취미는 한류 영화 감상이에요. 미키 씨는요?
My hobby is watching Korean movies. What about you, Miki?

2 Noun + 에도

Two particles in sequence is in the phrase, 역사에도 관심이 있어요. A particle 에 is immediately followed by another particle 도. 에is usually used as a time or location particle, and can also be used as an article indicating the source of action. 도 is a particle meaning "also" or "even."

언어학에도 관심이 있어요. 에 "in" 도 "also"
I am also interested in linguistics.
연극에도 관심이 있어요.
I am also interested in plays.
아침에도 녹차를 마셔요.
Even in the mornings, I drink green tea.

3 Noun + 이에요 (-예요) is an informal polite ending copula. The formal polite ending copular is -ㅂ/입니다.

편지이에요   This/that/it is a letter.
우산이에요.   It is an umbrella.

무궁화 꽃이에요. It is *Mugunghwa.*
Noun + 이/가 있다 expresses possession or the status of existence

관심이 있어요. I am interested in (my interst exists …)
반찬이 있어요. There is a side dish.
메뉴가 있어요. There is a menu.

연습 Practice

Noun + 는/은 요?

1. 오늘 학교에 가요. 빈센 씨는요?
   I am going to school. What about you, Vincent?
2. 제 취미는 테니스이에요. 밍밍 씨는요?
   My hobby is playing tennis. What about you, Ming Ming?
3. 지금 전철을 타요. 스즈키 씨는요?
   I am taking a train. What about you, Mr. Suzuki?
4. 어제 주사를 맞았어요. 김 선생님은요?
   I got a vaccine shot yesterday. What about you, Mr./Mrs./Ms. Kim?
5. 저는 괜찮아요. 사장님은요?
   I am fine. What about you, President?

Sequenced particles

1. 도서관학에도 관심이 있어요. I am also interested in library science.
2. 교과서에도 나와있어요. Such content is also in the textbook.
3. 그 슈퍼마켓에요 세일이 있어요? . Is that supermarket also having a sale?
4. 스위스에도 온천이 있어요? Are there also hot springs in Switzerland?
5. 샌프란시스코에도 눈이 와요? Does it also snow in San Francisco?

Noun + 이에요.

1. 중학교 삼 학년 교과서예요. This is a third year junior high school textbook.
2. 우등생이에요. He/she is an honor student.
3. 화원이에요. This is a flower garden.
4. 그는 유명한 작가예요. He/she is a famous writer.
5. 감기환자들이에요. They are patients with flu.

Noun + 이/가 있다 expresses possession or the status of existence

1. 한국 문화에 관심이 있어요. I am interested in Korean culture.
2. 반찬이 있어요. There is a side dish.
3. 메뉴가 있어요. There is a menu.
4. 공책이 있어요. There is a notebook.
5. 동전이 많이 있어요. There are a lot of coins.

응용 Utilization

1. What is your major? 전공이 무엇이에요?
2. What is your hobby? 취미가 무엇이에요?
3. What is *peobuk*? 페북이 무엇이에요?
4. What is *alba*? 알바가 무엇이에요?
5. When is your birthday? 생일이 언제에요?
6. I am majoring in international affairs.
   전공이 국제관계학이에요.
7. I am also interested in law. What about you, Susan?
   법학에도 관심이 있어요. 수잔 씨는요?
8. I am also interested in K-contents. 케이 콘텐츠에도 관심이 있어요.
9. That person is an actress. 저 분은 배우이에요.
10. My younger sister is a junior high school student.
    제 여자 동생은 중학생이에요.

List of titles related to majors in universities

간호학과	건축학과	건축공학과	게임학과	경영정보학과
경영학과	경제학과	경찰학과	관광학과	교육학과
국어교육과	국어국문학과	기계공학과	기독교학과	노어노문학과
농업경제학과	도서관학	독어독문학과	동물자원학과	문예창작학과
문헌정보학과	문화재보존학과	물리학과	법학 북한학과	불교학과
불어불문학과	사학과	사회학과	사회복지학과	산업공학과
생명과학과	세무학과	서어서문학과	섬유공학과	소방학과
수의학과	수학과	심리학과	수의학과	수학과
심리학과	식품영양학과	신학과	약학과	언어학과
에너지공학과	연극학과	영상학과	영어영문학과	일어일문학과
임상병리학과	자유전공학부	재료공학과	전기전자공학과	정치외교학과
조경학과	중어중문학과	지리학과	철학과	치의학과
커뮤니케이션학과	컴퓨터공학과	통계학과	특수교육과	한문학과
한의학과	항공운항학과	행정학과	화학과	

제 10과 🖊

택시로 갈까요?

Transportation

❖ 10. 택시로 갈까요?

A 오늘 오후에 특별 공연이 있어요.
This afternoon there is a special performance.

같이 갈까요?
Would you like to go together?

B 네. 같이 가요.
Yes. I would like to go together.

A 그럼, 빨리 갑시다. 시간 없어요.
Then, let's hurry. There is no time.

B 택시로 갑시다.
Let's go by taxi.

택시 안에서
Inside the taxi

C 어서 타세요.
Welcome.

어디까지 가세요?
Where are you going?

A 예술의 전당까지 가 주세요.
Please go to *Yesul-ui jeondang* (Seoul Art Center).

단어 Vocabulary

오늘	today
오후에	in the afternoon
에	time particle
특별 공연	special performance
있어요.	There is···, There are··· 있다 to exist Verb stem 있 + informal polite ending 어요.
같이	together
갈까요?	Shall we go? 가다 to go Verb stem 가 + future inquisitive ending ㄹ까요?
네.	"yes"
가요.	go, goes 가다 to go Verb stem 가 + informal polite ending 요?
그럼	then
빨리	quickly
갑시다.	Let's go. 가다 to go Verb stem 가 + propositive ending ㅂ시다

시간	time
없어요.	··· do not have··· ···does not have··· 없다 to not to have Verb stem 없 + informal polite ending어요?
택시로	by taxi
안에서	inside
어서 타세요.	"Please get in (into the taxi),"
어디까지	to where
가세요?	··· do you go? 가다 to go 가세요? Verb stem 가 + polite request question 세요?
예술의 전당까지	to *Yesul-ui jeondang* (Seoul Art Center)
가 주세요.	"Please go.." 가주다 Verb stem 가 + auxiliary verb 주다 가 주세요. Verb stem 가 + auxiliary verb 주다 + polite request form 세요.

▌문법 Grammar

1 Informal polite ending

There are two major spoken verb endings based on speech style. One is a formal polite ending which is Verb stem + ㅂ니다/습니다. Another is an infomal polite ending which is Verb stem + 아/어 요. The informal polite ending is used when you converse with people with whom you feel close. Dropping 요 will be a blunt form which can only be used between same age classmates or older siblings to younger siblings.

Level of speech

Formal polite 공부하십니까? 공부하십니다.
Informal polite 공부해요? 공부해요.
Blunt form   공부 해.

Verb stem + 아/어/여 요 is based on the vowel harmonization rule. When the stem of the verb ends with the bright vowels, 아 or 오, Verb stem + 아요 is applied. For all other vowels, the ending -어요 is added to verb stems. In the case of the verb, 하다 "to do," an informal polite ending 여 is added.

Vowel Harmonization

Verb stem ending with vowels	Combination informal polite ending 어/아/여 요	Contraction	Examples
아	-아요	아요	사다 to buy-사요
오	-아요	오+아요	오다 to come- 와요
어	-어요	어요	읽다 to read – 읽어요
우	-어요	우+어요-워요	덥다 to be hot – 더워요
으	-어요	으+어요-어요	쓰다 to write – 써요
이	-어요	이+여요-여요.	마시다 to drink – 마셔요
하	-여요	하+여요-해요	공부하다 to study- 공부해요

2 Action verb stem + ㄹ (을) 까요? is an ending for expressing "shall I…" or "shall we…" For descriptive verbs, the subject of the sentence becomes the third person, and the ending denotes a question, doubt, or polite denial.

With action verbs	집에 갈까요?　Shall we go home? 연필로 쓸까요? Shall I write in pencil? 보리차를 마실까요? Shall we have barley tea?
With descriptive verbs	영화가 재미있을까요? Do you think the movie will be interesting? 사람이 없을까요? Do you think there will be a lot of people? 날씨가 좋을까요? Do you think the weather will be nice?

3 Verb stem + (ㅂ) 시다 is a propositive form equivalent to "Let's ⋯"
교과서를 읽읍시다.　Let's read the textbook.
학교까지 갑시다.　　Let's go to school.
할아버지께 인사합니다. Let's greet grandfather.

4 Verb stem + (으)세요 is an ending for a polite request form.
지금 가세요.　Please leave now.
여기 보세요.　Please look here.
책을 읽으세요. Please read the book.
새해 복 많이 받으세요.　Happy New Year!

5 까지 means "all the way to" a certain destination or means "until"
어린이 대공원까지 가요.　I go all the way to Children's Park.
서점까지 가요.　I go all the way to the bookstore.
내일까지 레포트를 써요.　I am writing my term paper until tomorrow.

6 Action verb stem 가 + (아/어/여) 주다 is a combination of a main verb
가다and the auxiliary verb 주다. The auxiliary verb 주다 "to give or to
offer", in particular, supports the action of the main verb in favor of
the speaker. 가 주세요 means, "please go to ⋯.." for the speaker.

신문을 보여 주세요.   Show me the newspaper, please.

공항까지 가 주세요.   Take me to the airport, please.

가르쳐 주세요.   Please teach me.

▌연습 Practice

Informal polite ending - Verb stem + 아/어/여 요

1. 공연이 있어요. There is a performance.

2. 숙제를 해요. I am doing my homework.

3. 시간 없어요. There is not (enough) time.

4. 내일은 바빠요. I am busy tomorrow.

5. 월급이 적어요. My salary is low.

Verb stem + ㄹ 까요?

1. 종이접기를 배울까요? Shall we learn paper folding?

2. 여기 앉을까요? Shall we sit here?

3. 오늘도 바쁠까요? Would he/she also be busy?

4. 물어볼까요? Should we ask?

5. 팥빙수를 먹을까요? Shall we eat *patbingsu* (shaved ice)?

Verb stem + 시다

1. 저기까지 같이 뜁시다. Let's run to there.

2. 서두릅시다.   Let's hurry.

3. 먹읍시다.   Let's eat.

4. 봅시다.   Let's see.

5. 마십시다. Let's drink.

까지 to, all the way up, until

1. 어디까지 가세요? Where (where to) are you going?
2. 언제까지 기다려요? Until when are you waiting?
3. 내일까지 이 일을 다 마쳐야 합니다.

    I have to complete this work until tomorrow.
4. 이 책은 오늘 오후까지 도서관에 반납해야 합니다.

    I have to return this book until this afternoon.
5. 몇 시까지 갈까요?

    Until what time, should I go (to visit you or drop by)?

Action verb stem + 아/어/여 주다

1. 광화문 네거리까지 가 주세요.

    Please take me to the *Gwanwhamun* Intersection.
2. 문제를 풀어 주세요.

    Please solve this problem (for me).
3. 좋은 책을 소개 해 주세요.

    Please introduce a good book.
4. 이름을 여기에 써 주세요.

    Please write your name here.
5. 남대문까지 가는 길을 알려 주세요.

    Please tell me the way to *South Gate Nam*.

응용 Utilization

1. 일이 힘들어요. The work is hard.
2. 사무실이 어두워요. The office is dark.
3. 물을 마셔요. I am/he is/she is drinking water.
4. 이메일 보낼까요? Shall I send an e-mail?
5. 내일 날씨가 좋을까요? Do you think we will have good weather tomorrow?
6. 추울까요? Will it be cold?
7. 따뜻할까요? Will it be warm?

8. 오후까지 학교에 갑시다. Let' go to school by this afternoon.

9. 버스를 탑시다. Let's take a bus.

10. 같이 배웁시다. Let's learn together.

11. 거기 계세요? Are you there? (honorific for 있다 - 계시다)

12. 여기 보세요. Please look here.

13. 교과서 제3과를 읽으세요. Please read Lesson 3 in the textbook.

14. 서울에서 경주까지 몇 시간이 걸려요?

    How many hours will it take from Seoul to *Gyungju*?

15. 몇 시까지 기다려요? Until what time should I wait?

16. 쉬운 방법을 가르쳐 주세요. Please teach me an easy way.

17. 같이 가 주세요. Please come with me.

18. 도와주세요. Please help.

19. 안부 전해 주세요. Please send my regards.

20. 돌아서 가 주세요. Please go by turning around.

▌읽기 Reading

예술의 전당 포토존입니다.

사진을 어디에서 찍으면 좋을까요?

제11과 🖊

어떤 선물이 좋을까요?

Choosing a Gift

❖ 11. 어떤 선물이 좋을까요?

A 한국말 재미있어요?

Is the Korean language interesting?

B 재미있지만 어려워요.

It is interesting but it is difficult.

참, 내일 친구 생일이에요.

By the way, tomorrow is my friend's birthday.

어떤 선물이 좋을까요?

What kind of presents would be nice?

A 내일은 밸런타인데이이네요.

Tomorrow is Valentine's Day.

장미 꽃과 초콜릿은 선물로 좋을까요?

Would roses and chocolates be good as gifts?

B 좋은 생각이에요.

It is a good idea.

단어 Vocabulary

한국말	the Korean language
재미있어요?	Is it interesting? 재미있다 to be interesting 재미있어요? Verb stem 재미있 + informal polite inquisitive form 어요?
재미있지만	⋯ it is interesting but ⋯ 재미있다 to be interesting 재미있지만 Verb stem 재미있 + connective ending 지만

어려워요.	It is difficult.
	어렵다 to be difficult
	어려워요.
	    Verb stem 어려우 + (우+어→워) informal polite
	    inquisitive form 어요?

참	"by the way" This word is a colloquial interjection. When a speaker wants to change a topic of conversation or wants to be reminded by the self on a topic, 참 is used as an exclamatory interjection.
내일	tomorrow
친구	friend
생일	birthday
어떤 선물	what kind of present

좋을까요?	⋯ (You think) it would be good/nice to⋯.
	좋다 to be good/nice
	좋을까요?
	    Verb stem 좋 + inquisitive ending inquiring
	    someone's opinion ㄹ/을까요?

밸런타인데이	Valentine's Day
장미	rose
꽃	flower
초콜릿	chocolate
좋은 생각	nice idea/thought

105

문법 Grammar

1 Verb stem + (이)지만 is a connective ending which expresses a contrast to a prior act or fact which means "but," "however."

재미있지만 어려워요.
It is interesting but is difficult.
그 식당 불고기는 비싸지만 맛있어요.
Bulgogi at that restaurant is expensive but is delicious.
사무실은 넓지만 전철 역에서 멀어요.
My office is spacious but is far from the train station.

2 Action verb stem + ㄹ (을) 까요? is an ending for expressing "shall I⋯" or "shall we⋯" For descriptive verbs, the subject of the sentence becomes a third person, and the ending denotes a question, doubt, or polite denial.

어떤 꽃이 좋을까요? What kinds of flowers will be nice?
아직도 바쁠까요? Will he/she still be busy?
시간이 얼마나 남았을까요? How much time is left?

3 Noun + (으) 로 functions as an instrumental particle denoting means of an action used in phrases like "take or go by a taxi" or "as a gift."

생일 선물로 좋아요. It is good as a gift.
추억으로 남아요. It remains as a good memory.
호기심으로 배워요. I am learning out of curiosity.

4 Descriptive verb stem + ㄴ/은 functions as an adjectival when followed by a noun. Here is a break down of 좋은 생각 which means "a good idea/ thought."

좋다 to be good
　　좋 verb stem + 은 + Noun → 좋은 생각
바쁜 대학생 a busy college student
예쁜 꽃　　a pretty flower
작은 가방　a small bag

연습 Practice

Verb stem + (이)지만

1. 설명하시지만 모르겠습니다. You are explaining but I do not understand.
2. 거짓말이지만 재미있어요. It is fake but is interesting.
3. 아프지만 학교에 가겠어요. I am ill but will go to school.
4. 창문이 있지만 어두워요. There are windows but it is dark.
5. 메모리가 크지만 불편해요. It has large memory capacity but is inconvenient.

Descriptive verb stem + ㄹ/을까요?

1. 오후에 날씨가 좋을까요?

   Do you think the weather will be nice in the afternoon?
2. 그 책이 도서관에 있을까요?

   Do you think the book may be in the library?
3. 영화가 재미있을까요?

   Do you think the movie will be interesting?
4. 컴퓨터가 비쌀까요?

   Do you think the computer will be expensive?
5. 집에서 멀까요?

   Do you think the place will be far (from here)?

Noun + (으) 로

1. Would it be good as a wedding gift? 결혼 선물로 좋을까요?
2. I will pay in cash. 현금으로 내요.
3. It remains as a memory. 기억으로 남아요.
4. We find a photograph. 사진으로 찾아요.
5. Good habits lead a person to succeed. 좋은 습관으로 성공해요.

Descriptive verb stem + ㄴ/은

1. 작은 집 a small house
2. 큰 건물 a large building
3. 맛있는 곰탕 a tasty *Gomtang*
4. 맑은 하늘 clear sky
5. 노란 셔츠 a yellow shirt

1. It is interesting but it is difficult. 재미있지만 어려워요.
2. There are many people in the subway, but it is convenient.
   지하철에 사람이 많지만 편리해요.
3. There is a walking trail but I will stay here.
   산책로가 있지만 여기 있겠어요.
4. It is close to my place. 집에서 가까워요.
5. It will remain as a good memory. 좋은 추억으로 남아요.
6. Would this good as a birthday gift? 생일 선물로 좋을까요?
7. Should we go by airplaine? 비행기로 갈까요?
8. Should I speak in English? 영어로 말할까요?
9. He/she buys expensive watches. 비싼 시계를 사요.
10. It is an uncomfortable chair. 불편한 의자이에요.

읽기 Reading

선물 by 멜로망스

…남의 얘기 같던 설레는 일들이
내게 일어나고 있어
나에게만 준비된 선물 같아
자그마한 모든 게 커져만 가

항상 평범했던 일상도
특별해지는 이 순간 …

제12과 🖊

늦겠어요.

Being Late

❖ 12. 늦겠어요.

A 이 지하철은 서울역에 가지 않습니다.
This subway line does not stop at Seoul Station.

시청에도 안 가요.
It does not stop at City Hall either.

B 어떻게 하지요? 약속 시간에 늦겠어요.
What should I do? I will be late for my appointment.

단어 Vocabulary

지하철	subway
서울역	Seoul Station
가지 않습니다.	··· does not go 가다 to go 가지 않습니다 　Verb stem 가 + negative predicate 지 않다 + formal 　polite ending 습니다.
시청	Seoul City Hall
안 가요.	Conjugation for negating 안 + Verb stem 가 + informal polite 요
어떻게	how
약속	appointment
시간	time
늦겠어요.	··· will be late 늦다 to be late 늦겠어요. 　Verb stem 늦 + future infix 겠 + informal polite 　ending 어요.

▌문법 Grammar

1 Verb stem + 지 않다 is a conjugation for negation or negative predicate meaning "not." In spoken Korean, 안 as a negative predicate followed by verbs is often used for a simpler version of negation.

가다	to go
가지 않다	Verb stem 지 + negation 않다
가지 않아요.	Verb stem 지 + negation 않다 + informal polite 아요.

배우다	to learn
배우지 않아요.	Verb stem 지 + negation 않다 + informal polite 아요.
안 배워요.	안 Verb stem 배우 + informal polite (우+어 →워) 어요.

문제를 풀다	to solve problems
문제를 풀지 않아요.	Verb stem 문제를 풀다 + negation 지 않다 + informal polite 아요.
안 풀어요.	안 + verb stem 풀어 + informal polite 어요.

맵다	to be spicy
맵지 않다	Verb stem맵 + negation 지 않다
맵지 않아요.	Verb stem 맵 + negation 지 않다 + informal polite form아요
안 매워요.	안 + Verb stem 매 + informal polite form어요(우+어-워)

2 Verb stem + 겠 is a future tense infix which is equivalent to "…will…"

늦다	to be late
늦겠다	Verb stem 늦 + future infix 겠
늦겠어요.	Verb stem 늦 + future infix 겠 + informal polite ending 어요.

가다	to go
가겠다	Verb stem 가 + future infix 겠
가겠어요.	Verb stem 가 + future infix 겠 + infomal polite ending 어요
지금 가겠어요.	I will go now.

▌연습 Practice

Verb stem + 지 않다

1. 물건이 좋지 않아요. The item is not so good.
2. 마음에 들지 않아요. I do not like it.
3. 마음에 안 들어요.   I do not like it.
4. 눈이 오지 않아요.   It is not snowing.
5. 비가 안 와요.   It is not raining.

Verb stem + 겠

1. 만나겠어요. I will meet/see.
2. 설명하겠어요. I will explain.
3. 먹겠어요.   I will eat.
4. 강의를 듣겠어요. I will take a course.
5. 영화를 보겠어요. I will watch a movie.

▌응용 Utilization

1. It is not cloudy.
    흐리지 않아요. 안 흐려요.
2. I do not use Facebook.
    페이스북(페북)을 쓰지 않아요. 페북을 안 써요.
3. I am not reading that novel.
    그 소설은 읽지 않아요. 안 읽어요.
4. The snow is not falling.
    눈이 내리지 않아요. 눈이 안 내려요.
5. I do not need an umbrella.
    우산은 필요하지 않아요. 안 필요해요.
6. It is not difficult. 어렵지 않아요. 안 어려워요.
7. It will rain. 비가 오겠어요.
8. I will be bored. 심심하겠어요.
9. Roses will bloom. 장미가 피겠어요.
10. I will buy a ski suit. 스키복을 사겠어요.

한글날

Hangeul Day

❖ 13. 한글날

A 한글날이 언제이에요?
When is *Hangeul* Day?

B 10월 9일이에요.
It is October 9th.

A 내일 국립한글박물관에 가려고 해요.
I plan to visit the National *Hangeul* Museum.

B 몇 시에 가시겠어요?
What time will you go?

A 오후 한 시에요.
One o'clock in the afternoon.

B 한글박물관은 몇 시까지 해요?
Until what time does the *Hangeul* Museum open?

오늘은 금요일이니까 여섯시까지 해요.
Because today is Friday, they are open until six o'clock.

단어 Vocabulary

한글날	*Hangeul* Day is October 9.
언제	when
10월 9일	October 9th
내일	tomorrow
국립한글박물관	National *Hangeul* Museum
에	location particle "to"
몇 시	what time
오후	afternoon
오전	morning
한 시	one o'clock
까지	to
오늘	today
금요일	Friday 월요일 Monday 화요일 Tuseday 수요일 Wednesday 목요일 Thursday 금요일 Friday 토요일 Saturday 일요일 Sunday
Noun + 이니까	"because"
여덟 시	eight o'clock

1. 10월 9일 **is read as** 시월 구일

Cardinal Numerals

Korean has two sets of numbers: Korean numerals and Chinese numbers or Sino-Korean numbers. For the numerals 1~99 both sets are used. For the numbers 100 and up, the Sino-Korean numbers are used.

Korean numerals are used

시 시간 번 살 갑 사람 분 마리 권 채 대 개 자루 장

Sino-Koran numerals are used for minutes, years, currencies, building floors, and months. 분 년 원 층 월

Pure Korean numerals are used for counting days and for dates

하루 이틀 사흘 나흘 닷새 엿새 이레 여드레 아흐레 열흘

Sino-Korean numerals are for years, months, and days.

2022년 10 월 9 일

이천이십이년 시월 구일

Examples

Year 일 년, 이 년, 삼 년, 사 년, 오 년

Month 한 달, 두 달, 석 달, 넉 달, 다섯 달

Week 일주일, 이 주일, 삼주일, 사 주일, 오 주일

Month 일월, 이월, 삼월, 사월, 오월, 유월, 칠월, 팔월, 구월, 시월, 십 일월, 십 이월

Day 일일, 이일, 삼일, 사일, 오일, 육일, 칠일, 팔일, 구일, 십일

Hour 한 시간, 두 시간, 세 시간, 네 시간, 다섯 시간

Arabic	Korean numbers	Sino-Korean numbers
1	하나	일
2	둘	이
3	셋	삼
4	넷	사
5	다섯	오
6	여섯	육
7	일곱	칠
8	여덟	팔
9	아홉	구
10	열	십
20	스물	이십
30	서른	삼십
40	마흔	사십
50	쉰	오십
60	예순	육십
70	일흔	칠십
80	여든	팔십
90	아흔	구십
100	백	백

1,000 천 10,000 만   100,000,000 천만   100,000,000 억

2 Action verb stem + (으) 려고 "in order to"

- (으) 려고 is the suffix expressing a purpose of the action meaning "in order to." ― 려고 is the suffix after verb stems ending in a vowel, 으려고 is after verb stems ending in a consonant.

목욕을 하려고 해요. I intend to take a bath.
친구를 만나려고 해요. I intend to see my friend.
손을 씻으려고 화장실에 갔습니다. I went to a restroom to wash my hands.

3 몇 시에 가시겠어요? What time would you like to go?

가시겠어요? Would you like to go?

This ending can be broken down into three steps. Keep the verb stem and add the honorific infix, future infix, and informal polite ending.

가다   to go

가시다 Verb stem가 + honorific infix 시

가시겠다 Verb stem가 + honorific infix 시 + future infix 겠

가시겠어요. Honorific infix 시 + future infix 겠 + informal polite 어요.

학교에 오시겠어요?

Would you like to come to school?

영화를 보시겠어요?

Would you like to see a movie?

4 까지 "to" from - to 부터 - 까지

오전 부터 오후 까지 from morning to afternoon

여덟시 까지 to eight o'clock

여섯시 까지 to six o'clock

5 Verb stem + 이/니까 is a causal conjunctive ending meaning "because" or "so".

오늘은 금요일이니까 여덟시까지 해요.

Since today is Friday, they are open until eight o'clock.

겨울에는 추우니까 두꺼운 옷을 입어야 해요.

Because it is cold in winter, you have to wear heavy clothes.

여름에는 더우니까 땀이 많이 나요.

Because it is hot in summer, people perspire a lot.

몸이 아프니까 병원에 가야해요.

Because you are ill, you must go to hospital.

연습 Practice

1. 1월 1일 일월 일일 새해   New Year's Day
2. 3월 1일 삼월 일일 삼일절   March First Independence Day
3. 음력 4월 8일 부처님 오신 날 사월 팔일   Buddha's birthday
4. 추석 음력 8월 15일 팔월 십 오일   *Chuseok* August 15 by lunar calendar
5. 크리스마스 12월 25일 십 이월 십 오일   Christmas

Verb stem + (으) 려고 하다

1. 한국말을 공부하려고 한국에 가겠어요.
   I plan to go to Korea to study the Korean language.
2. 점심을 먹으려고 중국 식당에 가겠어요.
   I plan to go to a Chinese restaurant to have lunch.
3. 첫 기차를 타려고 일찍 일어납니다.
   I am getting up early to take the first train.
4. 책을 빌리려고 도서관에 갑니다.
   I plan to go the library to borrow books.
5. 일찍 일어나려고 시계를 맞추어 놓아요.
   In order to get up early, I am setting the alarm clock.

Verb stem + future infix 겠

1. 대답 하겠어요. I will answer.
2. 웹툰을 읽겠어요. I will read the online comics.
3. 사무실에서 자겠어요. I will sleep at the office.
4. 기숙사에 있겠어요. I will be at the dormitory.
5. 바나나를 먹겠어요. I will eat bananas.

Noun + 까지

1. 서울에서 부산까지   from Seoul to Busan
2. 여섯 시 부터 아홉 시 까지 from six to nine o'clock
3. 열 두시 까지   until twelve o'clock
4. 다섯 시 사십 오분 까지 until five forty five
5. 일곱 시 십 분 까지 until seven ten

Verb stem + (이) 니까

1. 주말이니까 조용해요.

   It is quiet because it is a weekend.

2. 오늘은 비가 오니까 집에 있겠어요.

   I am staying at home because it is raining today.

3. 그 가구는 싸니까 삽니다.

   I am buying this piece of furniture because it is cheap.

4. 피곤하니까 일찍 집에 들어갑니다.

   I am going home early because I am tired.

5. 위험하니까 조심하세요.

   Please be careful because it is dangerous.

▌응용 Utilization

1. My birthday is on January 19. 제 생일은 일월 십 구일입니다.
2. June 4   6월 4일 (유월 사일)
3. School begins from March 1. 개학은 3월 1일이에요. (삼월 일일)
4. Summer vacation is until August 31.
    여름 방학은 8월 31일까지 이에요. (팔월 삼십 일일)
5. The art museum is open until this afternoon.
    미술관은 오후까지입니다.
6. I finished the job so that I can leave work early.
    일찍 퇴근하려고 일을 마쳤어요.
7. I went to a bookstore to buy a book.
    책을 사려고 서점에 갔습니다.
8. I went to Insa Station to take a train.
    전철을 타려고 인사동 역으로 갔습니다.
9. I went to a post office to send a letter.
    편지를 붙이려고 우체국에 갔습니다
10. What time are you leaving?
    몇 시에 떠나시겠어요?

11. Will you be learning *Taekwondo*?
    태권도를 배우시겠어요?

12. Are you going to have Korean food?
    한식을 드시겠어요?

13. From London to Paris 런던에서 파리까지

14. From Tokyo to Hokkaido 동경에서 홋카이도까지

15. From three in the morning to midnight
    새벽 세 시 부터 밤 열 두시 까지

16. I cannot have a clear mind because there are too many people.
    사람들이 많으니까 정신이 없어요.

17. Because the mountain is high, we have a beautiful view.
    산이 높으니까 경치가 아름답습니다.

18. Because the movie is interesting, I would like see it again.
    영화가 재미있으니까 다시 보고 싶어요.

▍읽기 Reading

1월 1일	일월 일일
부처님 오신 날(음력 4월 8일)	음력 사월 팔일
크리스마스(성탄절, 12월 25일)	십 이월 이십 오일
개천절(10월 3일)	시월 삼일

한식 메뉴

한정식	20,000원	이만 원
설렁탕	9,000원	구천 원
곰탕	9,500원	구천 오백 원
된장찌개	6,000원	육천 원
김치찌개	5,500원	오천 오백원
갈비탕	7,000원	칠천 원

Extra reading 얼마예요?

피자 베니스 콤비네이션	13,500	만삼천오백원	18,000 만팔천원
피자 밀라노 스페셜	12,000	만이천원	10,000 만원
라이엔나 씨푸드	15,000	만오천원	17,000 만칠천원
샐러드	3,500	삼천오백원	
크림스프	2,500	이천오백원	
카레라이스	8,500	팔천오백원	
소프트웨어	1,135,037원	백십삼만오천삼십칠원	
지갑	119 달러	백십구 달러	
만년필	129 유로	백이십구 유로	
기차표	70 파운드	칠십 파운드	

몇 시부터 시작해요?

Weekly Schedule

❖ 14. 몇 시부터 시작해요?

A 몇 시부터 강의 들으세요?
From what time are you having a class?

B 아홉 시부터 시작해요.
It starts from 9:00.

A 무슨 강의인데요?
What course are you taking?

B 국제관계학이에요.
It is International Relations.

A 재미있겠어요.
It must be interesting.
구십분 강의인가요?

Is it a 90 minute lecture?

B 아니요. 백분 강의에요.
No, It is a 100 minute lecture.

A 그럼, 열 시 사십 분에 끝나나요?
Then, does it end at 10:40?

B 네. 강의가 끝나자마자 건축학 개론을 들어요.
Yes. As soon as the class is over, I will go to the Introduction to Architecture class.

월요일, 수요일, 금요일에는 한국어 수업이 있습니다.
I have a Korean class on Mondays, Wednesdays, and Fridays.

화요일 목요일에는 수업이 없습니다.
I do not have classes on Tuesdays and Thursdays.

단어 Vocabulary

몇 시부터	from what time
강의	lecture, class at a college, courses 강의를 듣다 to take a course 몇 시부터 강의를 들으세요? From what time does your class begin? 들어세요 comes from a ㄷ irregular verb 듣다 which is a dictionary from meaning 'to listen'
아홉 시부터	from 9 o'clock
시작해요.	It begins… 시작하다 to begin Verb stem 시작하 + informal polite ending 아요. (하+아→해)
무슨	what kind of
국제관계학	International Relations
재미있겠어요.	It must be interesting.
구십분	ninety mintues
강의인가요?	"I am not sure, but is it a lecture?" Verb stem 이 + ㄴ 가요? conjuctive ending for asking for an assurance "I am not sure but is it…"
아니요.	"No."

백분	100 minutes
그럼	a conjunction meaning "then"
열 시 사십 분	ten forty

끝나나요?	"May I ask whether it ends?"
	끝나다 "to end"
	끝나나요?
	   Verb ending 나요 is only used in a question form
	   for politely expressing doubt or politely asking
	   questions

끝나자마자	'as soon as it ends'
	끝나다 "to end"
	끝나자마자
	   Verb stem 끝나 + conjunctive ending meaning "as
	   soon as" 자마자

건축학 개론	Introduction to Architecture
한국어 수업	Korean language class

문법 Grammar

1 몇 what, how many
   몇 시 what time

Classifiers in Korean Korean numerals are used			
시	o'clock	마리	counting four legged animals or birds
시간	duration of time	권	classifiers for books or bounded items
번	counting frequency	채	Counting building structures
살	counting age	대	counting machines
갑	counting boxed items	개	generic counter for fruit or tangible objects
사람	counting people	자루	counting writing instruments
분	honorific classifier for counting people	장	counting pages
Sino-Koran numerals are used for minutes, years, currencies, floors, and months.			
분	minutes	층	floors
년	years	월	month
원	Korean money currency		

When telling time, Korean numbers for hours, and Sino-Korean numbers for minutes and seconds

오전 3시 15분 29초
세 시   십오분 이십구초

01:45   새벽 한 시 사십 오분
07:30   오전 일곱 시 삼십 분 or 일곱 시 반
12:28   오후 or 낮 열두 시 이십 팔 분

129

2   - 부터 from

입학식은 오후 두시 반 (두시 삼십 분) 부터 시작합니다.

The entrance ceremony will begin from 2:30 in the afternoon.

수업은 지금부터입니다.

There is a class from now.

콘서트는 오후 여섯 시부터입니다.

The concert is from six in the afternoon.

3   듣다 to listen or to hear ㄷ irregular

강의를 듣다 to take a class or course

뉴스를 듣다 listen to the news

The verb stem ending in ㄷ changes to ㄹ when a vowel is followed,
but ㄷ remains unchanged when a consonant is followed.

듣다 → 들어요.

Verb stem	AVS+는 DVS+은	VS+았/었	formal polite	VS + (으)면	VS + 기 Nominalizer
걷다 To walk	걷는	걸었어요	걷습니다	걸으면	걷기
깨닫다 To realize	깨달은	깨달았어요.	깨닫습니다	깨달으면	깨닫기
듣다 To listen	듣는	들었어요.	들었습니다.	들으면	듣기
묻다 To ask	묻는	물었어요.	물었습니다.	물으면	묻기
싣다 To load	싣는	실었어요.	실었습니다.	실으면	싣기

There are a list of ㄷ ending verbs which do not change.

닫다 to close   문을 닫습니다. I am closing the door.

받다 to receive   좋은 성적을 받았어요. I got good grades.

믿다 to trust   사장님만 믿어요.

                   I only trust the president (of a company).

쏟다 to pour/spill   아기가 우유를 쏟습니다. A baby spilled milk.
얻다 to gain   광고 회사에서 볼펜을 얻었습니다.
                      I got a ball point pen from an advertising company.

4 Verb Stem + 겠 is a future infix, and can also express a speaker's opinion when the verbs are descriptive. 재미있겠어요 would mean "it must be interesting."

비싸겠어요. I believe it must be expensive.
바쁘시겠어요. I believe you must be busy.
어렵겠어요. I believe it would be difficult.

5 Verb stem + ㄴ/은/는 가요? Interrogative ending used in asking questions in a polite way implying the speaker is not so sure of a particular place or circumstance.

구십 분 강의인가요?
(I am not so sure, may I ask, is it a 90 minute lecture?)
얼마인가요?
May I ask how much it is?
여기 사무실인가요? Is this place an office?

6 Verb stem + 나요 is only used in a question form for politely expressing doubt or politely asking questions

끝나다 to end
끝나나요? Verb stem 끝 + politely asking question 나요?

바쁘시나요?   Are you busy? (with a honorific infix 시)
시장 다녀오시나요? Are you coming from the market?
새 전화로 바꿔주나요? Will they exchange with a new phone?

7 그럼 is conjunction meaning, "well, then."

"그럼, 가족들은 어디 계세요? "
Well, then, where are your family members?
"그럼, 어떻게 가지요?"
Well, then how are we going?
"그럼, 얼마나 기다려요?"
Well, then how long do I need to wait?

8 Verb stem + 자마자 means "as soon as."

강의가 끝나자마자 운동하러 가요.
As soon as I am done with classes, I go for a workout.
집에 오자마자 전기불을 켜요.
As soon as I come home, I turn on the lights.
시디를 사자마자 클래식 음악을 들어요.
As soon as I buy CD flopply diskettes, I listen to classical music.

▌연습 Practice

17:15	오후 다섯 시 십오 분
22:48	밤 열 시 사십 팔 분
09:30	오전 아홉 시 삼십 분 (아홉 시 반)
12:00	낮 열두 시 (정오)
23:45	밤 열한 시 사십 오분

-부터

1. I am reading from this page.
   이 쪽부터 읽어요.
2. The class begins from eight in the morning.
   아침 아홉 시부터 시작해요.

3. All trains leave from Seoul Station.
서울역에서부터 떠나요.

4. I walk from the first floor to top.
일층에서 옥상까지 걸어가요.

5. I begin studying with the easy vocabulary.
쉬운 단어부터 공부하기 시작해요.

ㄷ irregular verb

1. 방탄소년단 노래를 들어요. I listen to BTS songs.
2. 이번 학기에 두 과목 듣습니다. I am taking two courses this semester.
3. 승객이 짐을 실어요. The passengers are loading their luggages.
4. 물어보세요. Please ask me.
5. 팟캐스트를 들어요. I am listening to podcasts.

Verb stem + 겠

1. 좋으시겠어요. You must feel good.
2. 예쁘겠어요.   It must be pretty.
3. 기쁘시겠어요. You must be pleased.
4. 맛있겠어요.   It must be delicious.
5. 비슷하겠어요   It must be similar.

Verb stem + (ㄴ) 가요?

1. 친절한가요? Is he/she kind?
2. 편리한가요? Is it convenient?
3. 다른가요?   Is it different?
4. 어려운가요? Is it difficult?
5. 조용한가요? It is quiet?

Verb stem + 나요?

1. 위험하나요? (May I ask whether) it is dangerous?
2. 중요하나요? (I am not sure but) is it important?

3. 편리하나요? (I am not sure but) is it convenient?

4. 편하나요? (I am not sure but) is it comfortable?

5. 아름답나요? (I am not sure but) is it beautiful?

Verb stem + 자마자

1. 수업이 끝나자마자 아르바이트를 해요.

   As soon as classes are over, I work part-time.

2. 집에 가자마자 목욕해요.

   As soon as I get to my place, I take a bath.

3. 졸업하자마자 취직해요.

   As soon as I graduate, I will get a job.

4. 회의가 끝나자마자 다른 회의를 해요.

   As soon as a meeting is over, there is another meeting.

5. 대답하자마자 또 질문해요.

   As soon as he/she answers, he/she asks questions.

▌응용 Utilization

1. From what time does your class begin?
   몇 시부터 수업을 시작해요?

2. I work part-time from five in the afternoon.
   오후 다섯 시부터 아르바이트에요.

3. How many courses are you taking this semester?
   이번 학기에 몇 과목 들으세요?

4. Where does it begin? 어디부터 시작해요?

5. When are you going to deliver? 언제 배달하는가요?

6. I would assume you must be busy. 바쁘시겠어요.

7. Please phone me as soon as you arrive at the station.
   역에 도착하자마자 전화해 주세요.

8. As soon as I sent the text messages, he/she contacted me.
   문자를 보내자마자 연락이 왔습니다.

9. As soon as the emergency exit was opened, I went out.
    비상구가 열리자마자 나갔습니다.

10. As soon as the iPhone came out, it was sold out.
    이 아이폰은 나오자마자 다 팔렸습니다.

▌읽기 Reading

월요일 오전에 한국어 수업이 있어요.

화요일 오후에 아르바이트를 해요.

수요일은 세미나 수업 후 연구회에 참석해요.

목요일 새벽에 라크로스 동아리 연습이 있어요.

금요일 저녁에는 학원에서 수학을 가르쳐요.

토요일에는 하루종일 운동을 해요.

일요일은 늦잠자고 아무것도 하지 않아요.

On a Korean Movie

건축학 개론 — Introduction to Architecture

There is a movie titled, 건축학 개론. The movie is a story about undergraduate classmates and their encounters with friends while taking Introduction to Architecture.

제15과 🖉

아침에 늦게 일어나세요?

Daily Schedule

❖ 15. 아침에 늦게 일어나세요?

A 학교에 오시지 않으면 아침에 늦게 일어나세요?
If you do not come to school, do you wake up late in the morning?

B 날마다 아침 일곱시 십분 전에 일어나요.
I wake up at ten to seven in the morning every day.

집에서 여덟시 십오분 전에 떠나요.
I leave my place at ten to eight.

그러면, 학교에 여덟시 반에 도착해요.
I arrive on campus at eight thirty.

벌써 아홉시이에요.
It is already nine o'clock.

빨리 가야겠어요.
I must hurry.

▌단어 Vocabulary

학교	School

오시지 않으면	···if you do not come to ···
	오다 to come
	오시다 Verb stem 오 + honorific infix 시
	오시지 않다 Verb stem 오 + honorific infix 시 + negation 지 않다
	오시지 않으면
	    Verb stem 오 + honorific infix 시 + negation 지 않다 + "if"
	    conjecture connective ending 으면

아침	in the morning
늦게	late
일어나세요?	Do you wake up?
날마다	everyday
일곱시 십분 전	ten minutes before seven o'clock
에	time particle "at"
일어나요	"I wake up." 일어나다 to wake up 일어나요 Verb stem + informal polite ending (어/아) 요

집에서는	from home – 에서 is a location particle attached to a noun. If an action has beginning and ending such as 공부하다 "to study," a location particle indicating where an act of studying begins and ends, 에서 is used. For example, "도서관에서 공부해요. I study at the library." In a sentence, "도서관에 가요. I am going to the library," 에 as a location particle indicating a particular place of destination is used.
여덟시 십오분 전	fifteen minutes before eight
떠나요.	떠나다 to leave 떠나요. Verb stem 떠나 + informal polite ending (어/아) 요
전	before
그러면	then
여덟 시 반	eight thirty
도착해요.	"I arrive" 도착하다 to arrive 도착해요. Verb stem 도착하 + informal polite ending 아요. (contraction해요)
지하철	subway
지하철 3호선	the subway line 3
타고	"I take a subway and…" 타다 to take (transportation), to ride Verb stem 타 + 고 "and / present progressive"
오지요.	"I come (for sure)." 오다 to come 오지요. Verb stem 오 + terminative ending 지요.
벌써	already
아홉시	nine o'clock
빨리	quickly
가야겠어요.	"must go" Verb stem 가 + connective "must"어/아/야 겠 + informal polite ending어요.

문법 Grammar

1 학교에 오시지 않으면 if you are not coming to school …

오다		dictionary form or verb stem
오시다	오 + 시	honorific infix
오시지 않다	오시 + 지 않다	negation
오시지 않으면	오시지 않 + 으면	conditional if ending

2 늦게 "late" as an adverb

늦다	to be late
늦게	늦 Verb stem +게 adverbial suffix

작다	to be small	
작게	small	소리를 작게 해 주세요. Please lower the sound volume

크다	to be big	
크게	big/large	크게 말씀 해 주세요. Please speak loudly.

따뜻하다	to be warm	
따뜻하게	warmly	따뜻하게 입으세요. Please dress warmly.

차다	to be cold	
차게	cold	우유를 차게 해 주세요. Please make this milk cold.

아름답다	to be beautiful	
아름답게	beautifully	그림을 아름답게 그려 주세요. Please paint beautifully.

3 에서 "from" or "at"

집에서 가까워요? Is it close to your place?
도서관에서 공부해요. I study at the library.
역에서 집까지 걸어서 가요. I walk from the station to my place.

4   그러면 "then"

여덟 시에 떠나요. 그러면 열 한시에 도착해요.

I leave at eight o'clock. Then, I will arrive at eleven o'clock.

산 정상까지 올라가세요. 그러면 보입니다.

Go all the way up to the top of the mountain. Then, you will see.

천천히 드세요. 그러면 소화가 잘 돼요.

Please eat slowly. Then, you will feel it is easier to digest.

5   Verb stem + 고 The ending is also used for connecting two actions. The English equivalent is "and."

지하철 3호선 타고 오지요.

타다 + 오다 - 타고 오다

   I come by taking the Subway Line 3. (I take the Subway Line 3 and come.)

   아침을 먹고 놀이터로 나갔어요.

   I had breakfast and went to the playground.

   겨울은 춥고 눈이 와요.

   In winter, it is cold and it snows.

6   Verb stem + 어/아 야 겠다. is an ending meaning "must."

가다	to go
가야겠다.	Verb stem 가 + must 야 + future infix 겠
가야겠어요.	Verb stem 가 + must 야 + future infix 겠 + Informal polite ending 어요

1. 학교에 오시지 않으면

   If you do not come to school, do you get up late?

2. 지금 가시지 않으면 후회합니다.

   If you do not go now, you will regret.

3. 연락하시지 않으면 예약 못 해요.

   If you do not contact the venue, you cannot make a reservation.

4. 교실에 계시지 않으면 그들이 찾지 못 합니다.

   If you are not in the classroom, they will not be able to find us.

5. 담배를 끊으시지 않으면 건강이 위험해요.

   If you do not quit smoking, your health will be at risk.

Verb stem + 게

1. 늦게 주무셨어요? Did you sleep late?
2. 문제가 쉽게 나왔어요. The exam had easy questions.
3. 맵게 양념했어요. It is seasoned with hot spices.
4. 짜게 해 주세요. Please make it salty.
5. 상처가 깊게 났어요. The wound is deep.

Location + 에서

1. 박물관에서 특별 전시를 하고 있어요.

   The museum is having a special exhibition.

2. 운동장에서 테니스 시합을 합니다.

   We are playing tennis at the playground.

3. 대학에서 경제학을 공부해요.

   I am studying economics at college.

4. 영화관에서 팝콘을 먹었어요.

   I had popcorn at the movie theater.

5. 연구실에서 토론을 했어요.

   We had a discussion at the office.

   사무실 is a generic term for office

   연구실 literally means research office.

Verb stem + 고

1. 자동차를 타고 학교에 옵니다.

   I come to school by car.
2. 엘리베이터를 타고 옥상까지 가요.

   I take an elevator up to the rooftop.
3. 마트에서 음식을 사고 집으로 와요.

   I come home after buying food from the (big chain of) discounted grocery stores.
4. 빨래를 하고 청소를 합니다.

   I wash clothes and clean the room.
5. 학생을 만나고 얘기를 들었습니다.

   I met students and heard the story.

Verb stem + 아/어 야겠어요.

1. 지금 이메일을 보내야겠어요.

   I should send an e-mail now
2. 건강에 조심해야겠어요.

   I should be careful with my health.
3. 기다려야겠어요.

   I must wait.
4. 고양이를 보살펴야겠어요.

   I must take care of the cat.
5. 알려드려야겠어요.

   I should let him/her know.

응용 Utilization

1. If you are coming to school, where do you study?
   학교에 오시지 않으면 어디에서 공부합니까?

2. If you are not tired, would you like to work out with me?
   피곤하지 않으면 같이 운동하실까요?

3. If you do not take a train, you will be late.
   전철을 타시지 않으면 늦습니다.

4. Would you please lower the audio?
   소리를 작게 해 주세요.

5. I was treated without pain.
   아프지 않게 치료했어요.

6. I practiced at the swimming pool.
   수영장에서 연습합니다.

7. You cannot smoke at the restaurant.
   식당에서 담배를 피지 못 해요.

8. Do you have time? Then, please help us.
   시간 있어요? 그러면 저희를 도와주세요.

9. Go ahead by car first. Then, we will leave later.
   차로 먼저 가요. 그러면 나중에 가겠어요.

10. Throw a ball. Then, I will catch it.
    공을 던져요. 그러면 제가 받아요.

11. I got off the bus, and changed to the subway.
    버스에서 내리고 지하철로 갈아탔습니다.

12. I read the newspapers, and left.
    신문을 읽고 떠났어요.

13. I must prepare for dinner.
    저녁 준비를 해야겠어요.

14. I must finish the term paper quickly.
    레포트를 빨리 마쳐야겠어요.

15. I must buy a pair of hiking shoes.
    등산화를 사야겠어요.

읽기 Reading

빈센의 아침

아침에 일어나자마자 세수하고 옷을 입는다. 그리고 커피를 마신다. 커피는 동네 카페에 가서 마신다. 매일 메뉴를 본다. 아메리카노는 4,500원, 카푸치노는 5,000원, 카페라떼 5,300원이다. 주로 카푸치노를 주문한다.

About Written Korean

Up to this point, we learned spoken formal polite and informal polite verb endings. Besides verb endings in the spoken Korean, there is written Korean verb ending used in any official context such as in delivering a speech or a presentation. The written Korean is also used in newspapers or in academic writing. Compared to the spoken verb endings, there are few written verb endings.

The Written Korean Verb Endings: Present tense

Action Verb 공부하다	Without *Batchim*	Verb Stem + ㄴ다	공부한다.
읽다	With *Batchim*	Verb Stem + 는다	읽는다.
Adjectival Verb 아름답다		Verb Stem + 다	아름답다.

Spoken Korean	Written Korean
Formal polite 공부합니다. Informal polite 공부해요.	공부한다.
Formal polite 아릅답습니다. Informal polite 아름다워요.	아름답다.
Formal polite 교과서입니다. Informal polite 교과서 이에요	교과서 이다.
Formal polite 도서관에 있습니다. Informal polite 도서관에 있어요	도서관에 있다.

In spoken Korean, there are formal polite and informal polite verb endings. Depending on the addressee that the speaker is conversing with, either formal or informal polite endings are used. Formal polite verb endings are used in official public announcements, formal speeches, news, or when making presentations. Informal polite ending is usually used in a daily conversation. A blunt form verb ending without 요 can only be used between close friends or family members of the same age or in informally consented to situations.

Written Korean has different verb endings. Written Korean verb endings are Verb Stem + ㄴ다 for the stem ending in vowels, Verb Stem + 는다 for the stem ending with consonants, and Verb Stem + 다 for adjectives. Written verb endings are used for any official purpose such as in public announcements, academic writings, or in newspapers. In novels, both written and spoken Korean are used when a passage includes a dialogue between two individuals.

> Examples

Spoken formal polite verb ending: News
오늘 뉴스를 전해드리겠습니다. 여기는 한국 은행 앞입니다.

Spoken informal polite verb ending:　Texting or daily conversation
레인 씨, 내일 시간 있어요? 같이 공연 보러 가요.

Spoken blunt form: Between close friends
어디 가? 좀 기다려.

Written verb ending: Academic writings, essays, or daily journal writing
　올해는 졸업 논문을 <u>쓴다</u>.
　한류 콘텐츠에 관심이 <u>있다</u>.
　한복은 <u>아름답다</u>.

Written verb ending: Newspaper

부동산 값이 급격히 오르고 <u>있다</u>. 주 원인은 많은 사람들이 투자하기 때문<u>이다</u>.

Written and spoken verb endings: An excert from a novel.

"불고기가 맛있어요. 맛있는 파전도 먹어요."

종석은 듣지 않고 책만 <u>읽는다</u>.

제 16과 🖊

재미있는 드라마를 봤어요.

Last Week

❖ 16. 재미있는 드라마를 봤어요.

A 사랑의 불시착이라는 드라마 보셨어요?
Did you see a drama titled, "Crash Landing"?

B 네. 봤어요.
Yes. I saw.

재미있는 드라마였어요.
It was an interesting drama.

드라마 보고나서 친구하고 맛있는 치킨을 먹었어요.
After seeing the drama with my friends, we ate tasty fried chicken.

그리고, 따뜻한 차와 커피를 마셨어요.
And, we had hot tea and coffee.

주인공이 맑은 하늘, 높은 산 아래에 있는 장면이 좋았어요.
We liked the scene where a main character was under a clear sky on high mountain.

단어 Vocabulary

사랑의 불시착	The title of a movie Crash of Love 사랑love 불시착crash landing Noun + 이라는 ".. so called" "titled"
드라마	drama

보셨어요?	Did you see?
	보다 to see
	보시다 Verb steam보 + honorific infix 시
	보시 + 였
	  Verb steam보 + honorific infix 시 + past tense 였 (시+였
	  → 셨 contraction)
	보셨+어요
	  Verb steam보 + honorific infix 시 + past tense 였 +
	  informal polite ending?

네.	Yes

봤어요.	"I saw…"
	  보다 to see
	  보 + 았다 Verb stem 보 + past tense 았(보 + 았 → 봤)
	  보았어요. or 봤어요. 봤+informal polite 어요.

재미있는	interesting
친구하고	with a friend or friends
맛있는	tasty, delicious
치킨	chiken usually indicating fried chiken
을	object particle which modifies verbs

먹었어요.	먹다 To eat
	먹었다
	  먹+었 Verb stem 먹 + past tense 었
	먹었어요
	  먹었 +어요 Verb stem 먹 + past tense 었 + informal polite 어요.

그리고	conjuctive, means "and"
따뜻한 차	hot tea
와/과	"and"
커피	coffee
을/를	object particle

마셨어요.	마시다 to drink
	마셨다
	마시+였다 Verb stem 마시 + past tense infix 였
	마셨+어요
	  Verb stem마시 + past tense infix 였(시+였→셨contraction)
	  + informal polite ending 어요

주인공	the main character
맑은	clear
하늘	sky
높은	high 높다 to be high 높은 Verb stem 높 + ㄴ/은
산	mountain
아래	under
에	location particle
있는 장면	a scene which exist … 있다 to exist 있는 Verb stem + adjectival ㄴ/은 + noun
좋았어요.	"was good" 좋다 to be good 좋+ 았다 past tense - 좋았 + 어요. informal polite ending

문법 Grammar

1 Noun + 이라는 "so called"

Have you heard a K-pop singer called "Black Pink?"
블랙핑크라는 케이팝 가수 들어봤어요?

Did you see a Korean movie titled "Winter Sonata"?
겨울 소나타라는 영화 보셨어요?

A person named Shao telephoned.
샤오라는 분한테서 전화왔어요.

2 Past tense formation -았/었/였 are past tense infix. Here is an example of how past tense endings can be conjugated.

보다	to see
보시다	Verb stem 보 + honorific infix 시
보셨다	Verb stem 보 + honorific infix 시 + past tense infix 였 (시+였→셨)
보셨어요?	Verb stem 보 + honorific infix 시 + past tense 였 + informal polite form 어요

보다	to see
보+았다	Verb stem 보 + past tense 았
봤다	contracted from of 보았다 → 봤다.
봤어요.	Verb stem 보 + past tense 았 + informal polite form 어요

Past tense infix -았/었/였 are based on the vowel harmonization rule. For example, 가다 which is a dictionary form or a verb stem 가 ends with a vowel ㅏ which is a positive or *yang* phoneme. When a past tense infix if applied to a bright vowel, 았 will be added to the verb stem. 어 in contrast to 아 is a dark or a symbol of *yin* vowel, the past tense infix will be 었.

Verb stem	Past infix	Past form	Contraction
가다	– 았	좋았어요	
많다		많았어요	
보다		보았어요	봤어요
오다		(오+았어요)*	왔어요.
가르치다		(가르치+었어요)	가르쳤어요
배우다		(배우+었어요)	배웠어요
있다	–었–	있었어요	
주무시다		(주무시+었어요)	주무셨어요
재미있다		재미있었어요	
감사하다	–였–	(감사하+였어요)	감사했어요.
공부하다		(공부하+였어요)	공부했어요
좋아하다		(좋아하+였어요)	좋아했어요
하다		(하였+어요)	했어요

* ( ) is to show the process prior to contracted form. What is written in the parenthesis is not actually used. It shows how the contraction resulted.

3 Action verb stem + 는

Verb stem + 는 is a modifier attached exclusively to action verbs. Adding 는to action verbs indicates something ongoing or an action in progress. Also, action verb stem + 는 becomes an adjective.

재미있다 to be interesting
재미있는 Action verb stem + 는
재미있 + 는 Action verb + 는 noun modifier or an adjective.

가르치는 선생님 a teacher who is teaching
공부하는 학생   a student who is studying
받는 사람   a person who is receiving

보내는 사람   a person who is sending

오는 사람   a person who is coming

4 Descriptive verb stem + ㄴ/은

Descriptive verb stem + ㄴ/은 is ending for noun modifiers or adjectives which precede nouns. ㄴ/은is attached to a descriptive verb stems or copula, which it expresses facts or current state of action or phenomenon.

바쁘다 to be busy - 바쁜 학생 busy student

맑다 to be clear - 맑은 하늘 clear sky

높다 to be high - 높은 산 a high mountain

Action verb stem ㄴ/은 refers to the past tense when attached to the action verb, it refers to the past tense

읽은 책   a book I read

본 사람   a person I saw

조금 전에 쓴 이메일을 보냈습니다. I sent an e-mail a few minutes ago.

잃은 물건을 찾았습니다. I found the lost item.

Verb stem + ㄴ/은 Noun + 이다

ㄴ/은 can also be attached to the copula which refers to the current state.

마음이 좋은 주인공입니다.

He/She is the main character with a good heart.

봄이 되면 노란 개나리가 핍니다.

When spring comes, yellow forsythia blooms.

이 분은 제 친구인 유리입니다.

This is my friend Yuri. (This is Yuri, who is my friend.)

In the case of the verb "to exist" 있다 "verb stem + 는" can be used as an adjective. In this phrase 아래에 있는 - 있다 is used as an adjective which modifies the noun.

높은 산 아래에 <u>있는</u> 장면

⋯ the scene under the high mountain

책상 위에 있는 것이 무엇이에요?

What is that on the desk?

그 앱은 없는 것이 좋겠어요.

It is better not to have that application.

5 Verb stem + 고 나서 after …ing

먹고 나서 잤습니다.

After having a meal, I slept.

아프고 나서 머리가 빠졌어요.

I lost my hair after being ill.

말하고 나서 후회했어요.

I regretted it after saying it (something I should not have said).

결혼하고 나서 알았어요.

I learned (knew) about it after getting married.

연습하고 나서 무대에 나갔어요.

After practicing, I went to the stage.

6 Noun 와/과 Noun "and"

와 nouns ending in vowels

과 nouns ending in consonants

따뜻한 차와 커피	hot tea and coffee
강아지와 고양이	a puppy and a cat
책과 교과서	a book and a textbook

연습 Practice

1. Noun + (이) 라는 "so called"

1. 무정이라는 소설 아세요?   Do you know a novel called, *Mujeong?*
2. 타로 사주라는 카페 아세요? Do you know a café called *Tarot Horoscope?*
3. 파솔리니라는 이탈리아 시인 아세요? Do you know an Italian poet called *Pasolini?*
4. 기생충이라는 영화 보셨어요? Did you see a movie called *Parasite?*
5. 추억이라는 수필을 읽었습니다. I read an essay titled, *Chueok.*

2. Past tense formation −았/었/였

1. 주말에 공부했어요. I studied over the weekend.
2. 영화가 재미있었어요. The movie was interesting.
3. 날씨가 좋았어요. The weather was very nice.
4. 가셨어요?   Did you go? (honoriic infix 시)
5. 지난 주는 아팠어요.   I was ill last week.

3.

(1) Action verb stem + 는

보내는 사람   a person who is sending
받는 사람   a person who is receiving
재미있는 과목   an interesting course
한국말을 배우는 학생 a student who is learning Korean
노래하는 가수   a singer who is singing

(2) Descriptive verb stem + ㄴ/은

비싼 책 expensive book
더운 날씨 hot weather
추운 밤   cold night
따뜻한 보리차 warm barley tea
무거운 돌 heavy stone

157

제16과 **재미있는 드라마를 봤어요.**

(3) Action verb stem ㄴ/은

조금 전에 쓴 이메일   an e-mail I wrote a few minutes ago
어제 읽은 소설 a novel I read yesterday
작년에 본 영화 a movie I saw last year
기억난 이름   a name which I remember/recall
아침에 먹은 빵   a piece of bread I had in the morning

(4) ㄴ/은 Noun + 이다

이 분은 제 친구인 유리입니다.

  This is Yuri who is my friend. (분: honorific infix for a person)
잃은 물건입니다. This is a lost item.
찾은 물건이에요. It is an item I found.
맑은 하늘입니다. It is a clear sky.
맛있는 한식이에요. It is a delicious Korean dish.

(5) Verb stem 있 + 는

높은 산 아래에 있는 장면을 기억해요.
I remember the scene which is under the high mountain.
책상 위에 있는 것이 무엇이에요?
What is the item that is on the desk?
공원에 있는 아이들입니다.
They are children who are playing at the park.
한강은 도시에 있는 강입니다.
The *Han River* is in a city.
이것이 동네에 있는 슈퍼마켓이에요.
This is a supermarket in the neighborhood.

4. Verb stem + 고 나서 after ...ing

드라마를 보고 나서 울었어요. After watching a drama, I cried.
말하고 나서 후회했어요. I regretted it saying that (which I should not have said).

결혼하고 나서 알았어요. After I got married, I knew (about something I did not know before).

연습하고 나서 무대에 나갔어요. After practicing, I went on stage.

화상회의를 하고 나서 산책했어요. After having a video conference, I went for a walk.

┃응용 Utilization

1. Do you know a youtuber called "*Seojun*"? 서준이라는 유튜버 아세요?
2. I saw a movie called "*Chunhwangjeon*." 춘향전이라는 영화를 봤어요.
3. Do you recall a book titled "*Time Goes*"? 지나가는 시간이라는 책 기억하세요?
4. I studied over the weekend.　주말에 공부했어요.
5. The movie was interesting.　영화가 재미있었어요.
6. The weather was very nice.　날씨가 좋았어요.
7. Did you go? 갔어요? Without a honorific infix
　　　　　 가셨어요? With a honorific infix
8. I met him/her on a rainy day. 비 오는 날에 만났습니다.
9. This is a bestselling book which selling a lot lately.
　요즘 베스트셀러로 팔리는 책입니다.
10. There are many students who are learning Korean.
　한국말을 배우는 학생이 많아졌습니다.
11. Today is a muggy day. 오늘은 무더운 날입니다.
12. They are customers who are waiting. 기다리는 손님입니다.
13. I sent an e-mail few minutes ago.
　조금 전에 쓴 이메일을 보냈습니다.
14. My sister who is working for a company 회사에 다니는 언니
15. This is my friend Kiara. 제 친구인 키아라입니다.
16. This is the item I lost.　이것이 제가 잃은 물건입니다.
17. This is a spicy *Tteokbokki*. 매운 떡볶이에요.
18. The scene which is under a high mountain 높은 산 아래에 있는 장면
19. What is it that is inside of the bag? 가방 안에 있는 것이 무엇이에요?
20. After I paid by credit card, I received the receipt.
　카드로 계산하고 나서 영수증을 받았어요.

159

제16과 재미있는 드라마를 봤어요.

21. After I downloaded a Japanese guide application, I did city sight seeing.
일본어 안내서 앱을 다운받고 나서 시내 구경했어요.
22. I ate *Dakgalbi* and had a shaved with ice bean. (*Patbinsu*)
닭갈비 먹고 나서 팥빙수를 먹었어요.
23. A pencil and a fountain pen 연필과 만년필
24. Wet tissue and sanitizer spray 물티슈와 소독용 스프레이
25. Roses and cake 장미와 케이크

▌읽기 Reading

사랑의 불시착(*From the drama Crash Landing on you*)

세상 어느 곳에 있더라도
 Even if it is anywhere in the world ⋯
어디라도 내가 찾아갈게.
 It may be anywhere, I will look for you.

어제 읽은 소설

Reading Books

❖ 17. 어제 읽은 소설

A 저는 한국 소설 책을 좋아해요.
I like Korean novels.

어제 읽은 시나리오 책은 도서관에서 빌렸어요.
I borrowed a movie script that I read yesterday.

한국어로 쓰였어요.
It is written in Korean.

B 시나리오도 도서관에 있군요.
The library even has movie scripts.

A 네. 도서관에 책이 많아요.
Yes, there are many books in the library.

오늘 읽는 소설 제목은 수진과 메타버스이에요.
The title of the novel I am reading today is *Sujin and Metaverse*.

요즘 MZ세대가 좋아해요.
Such novels are what the MZ generation likes.

그 소설은 상, 하로 나왔어요.
The novel came out in Volume I and Volume II.

내일 읽을 책은 하권이에요.
The book I will be reading is Volume II.

인스타그램에 올릴 거예요.
I am going to post it on Instagram.

단어 Vocabulary

저	the first person singular humble form "I". When referring to yourself to another, a humble form 저 will be proper. 나 is a generic first person singular meaning "I"
한국 소설	Korean novel
책	book
좋아해요.	"I like it." 　좋아하다 to like 　좋아해요 Verb stem 좋 + informal polite ending (하+아→해) 요.
어제	yesterday
읽은	read as a past tense modifier
시나리오 책	a scenario book which I read yesterday
도서관	library
–에서	at
빌렸어요.	borrowed 빌리다 to borrow 빌렸다　Verb stem 빌리 + past tense 였 (리+였→렸) 빌렸어요.　Verb stem 빌리 + past tense 였 + 　　informal polite ending 어요.

한국어로 쓰였어요.	It is written in Korean. 쓰다 to write 쓰이다 Verb stem + passive suffix 이 쓰였다 Verb stem + passive suffix 이 + pass tense infix였 쓰였어요. 쓰였+ informal polite ending 어요
시나리오	scenario, movie script
도	adverb meaning "also"
–에	location particle
있군요.	Verb stem있 + 군요 is terminative verb ending confirming or seeking agreement on a fact or a state of affairs
많아요.	많다 to be many "There are many …" Verb stem 많 + informal polite ending 아요.
오늘	today 오늘 읽는 책 the book I am reading today
제목	title
수진과 메타버스	*Sujin and Metaverse*
요즘	these days
MZ세대	MZ generation M stands for Millennials and Z stands for the young people born between the late 1990s and the early 2000s.
상, 하	상 means up 하 means low. When the words are referring to novels, 상 refers to Volume I and 하 for Volume II.
로	"as"
나왔어요.	"It came out." 나오다 to come out 나왔다 Verb stem 나오+ past tense infix 았(오+ 았→왔) 나왔어요. 나왔+ informal polite ending 어요.
내일	tomorrow
읽을 책	the book I will read

인스타그램	Instagram
올릴 거에요.	올리다 to raise, to post Verb stem ㄹ(을) 것이에요 conjugation for probable future The contracted form of 올릴것이에요.

문법 Grammar

1   저는 한국 소설 책을 좋아해요. I like Korean novels.

좋다 means "to be good"
좋아하다 means "to like"

저는 서울이 좋아요.　　　I like Seoul.
저는 태권도를 좋아해요.　I like *Taekwondo*.

2   빌렸어요 빌리+ past tense 였(리+였→렸) + informal polite ending 어요.

빌리다 to borrow
빌렸다 Verb stem 빌리 + past tense 였 (리+였→렸)
빌렸 Verb stem + past tense 였 (리+였→ 렸) + informal polite ending 어요.

3   쓰였어요 comes from a passive verb deriving from 쓰다. In Korean, there are four major passive verb suffixes, 이, 히, 리, 기.
쓰였어요 means "it is written …" comes from the verb 쓰다 "to write."
한국어로 쓰였어요 means "it is written in Korean."

쓰다 to write
쓰이다 Verb stem + passive suffix 이
쓰였다 Verb stem + passive suffix 이+ past tense infix였
쓰였어요. 쓰였+ informal polite ending 어요

		Passive Suffix
Verb stem + 이	보다	보이다 to be seen – 불을 켜니까 보입니다.
	놓다	놓이다 to be placed – 컴퓨터가 책상 위에 놓여있어요.
	쓰다	쓰이다 to be written – 한국어로 쓰였어요.
Verb stem + 히	닫다	닫히다 to be closed – 문이 닫혔어요.
	묻다	묻히다 to be buried – 여기에 묻혔어요.
	잡다	잡히다 to be caught – 범인이 잡혔어요.
	읽다	읽히다 to be read – 이제 잘 읽힙니다.
Verb stem + 리	듣다	들리다 to be heard – 잘 들려요.
	열다	열리다 to be opened – 열립니다.
	팔다	팔리다 to be sold – 집이 팔렸어요.
Verb stem + 기	끊다	끊기다 to get cut off – 전기가 끊겼어요.
	빼앗다	빼앗기다 to be stolen – "빼앗긴 들에도 봄은 오는가"
	씻다	씻기다 to get washed – 강아지를 씻겼어요.

4 도 "also"

시나리오도 도서관에 있군요.

The library even has movie scripts.

이 영화도 재미있어요.

This movie is also interesting.

모하메드도 한국말 잘 해요.

Mohamed also speaks Korean well.

5 Modifiers with action verbs and verb tenses include past, present, and future tense conjugations. In 읽은 소설 , 읽은 modifies the noun 소설 "a novel." Action verb stem + 는 used only with action verb, refer to the present tense Verb Stem + ㄴ/은 is used with both action verbs which refers to the past tense, It is used with descriptive verbs, and refers to the past tense.

Action/ Descriptive verb stem + ㄹ/을 is used with action verbs as well as with descriptive verbs, and is referred to the future meaning "that someone will do/action," "that will be/descriptive."

어제 읽은 소설   the novel I read yesterday
오늘 읽는 소설   the novel I am reading today
내일 읽을 소설   the novel I will read tomorrow

Modifiers with action verbs and verb tenses

	Past			Present		Future
Verb stem with *batchim*	Verb stem without *batchim*	Verb stem with *batchim*	Verb stem without *batchim*	Verb stem with *batchim*	Verb stem without *batchim*	
-은	-ㄴ	-는	-는	-을	-ㄹ
읽은	간	읽는	가는	읽을	갈

Action verb stem + 는 is used only with action verbs, and refers to the present tense meaning "the person/ thing that is doing something."

공부하는 사람은 유학생이에요.
The person who is studing is an overseas student.
책을 읽는 학생은 유미에요.
The person who is reading the book is Yumi.
일기 쓰는 습관이 있어요.
I have a habit of writing a daily journal.

Verb Stem + ㄴ/은 is used with action verbs, and refers to the past tense. It is also used with descriptive verbs, and refers to the past tense.
읽은 책 the book I read
본 사람 the person who I saw
경제를 공부한 대학생 a colleage student who studied economics

Action/ Descriptive verb stem + 르/을 is used with action verbs as well as with descriptive verbs which refers to the future meaning "that someone will do/action that will be…"

결혼할 사람이 김 대표이에요.
President Kim is the one who is going to get married.
이 앱이 좋을지 나쁠지 모르겠어요.
I do not know if this application will be good or bad.
쓰고 갈 우산을 샀어요.
I bought an umbrella which I will use.

Verb Modifiers

Dictionary Form	Past V + (으)는	Present V+는	Future V+(으)ㄹ/을
가다	간 곳	가는 곳	갈 곳
나오다	나온 사람	나오는 사람	나올 사람
노래하다	노래한 가수	노래하는 가수	노래할 가수
닫다	닫은 문	닫는 문	닫을 문
먹다	먹은 음식	먹는 음식	먹을 음식
보다	본 드라마	보는 드라마	볼 드라마
쓰다	어제 쓴 글	오늘 쓰는 글	내일 쓸 글
읽다	읽은 소설	읽는 소설	읽을 소설
입다	입은 옷	입는 옷	입을 옷
자다	어제 잔 시간	자는 시간	잘 시간
찾다	찾은 시계	찾는 시계	찾을 시계
하다	공부한 과목	공부하는 과목	공부할 과목

-을/를 좋아해요.

1. 사과를 좋아해요.   I like apples.
2. 단편 소설을 좋아해요. I like short stories.
3. 자동차를 좋아해요.   I like cars.
4. 유튜브 보는 것을 좋아해요. I like to watch YouTube.
5. 정치학 과목을 좋아해요. I like a political science course.

-에서

1. 도서관에서 공부해요.   I study at the library.
2. 교실에서 점심을 먹었어요. I had lunch in the classroom.
3. 산에서 캠핑을 했어요.   I went for camping in the mountains.
4. 식당 앞에서 기다립니다. I am waiting in front of the cafeteria.
5. 학원에서 중국어를 배워요.

   I am learning Chinese at *hakwon* (a type of private learning school).

Action verb stem + ㄴ/은 + Noun

1. 어제 읽은 소설 a novel I read yesterday
2. 지난 주에 간 서점 a bookstore which I visited last week
3. 작년에 공부한 과목 a course I took last year
4. 삼 년 전에 산 전자사전 an electronic dictionary I bought three years ago
5. 잃어버린 열쇠 a key I lost

Action verb stem + (으)는 + Noun

1. 오늘 읽는 소설 a novel I am reading today
2. 지금 쓰는 핸드폰 a cellphone which I am using now
3. 지금 마시는 우유 milk I am now drinking
4. 하늘을 날으는 연 a kite flying in the sky
5. 읽는 책 a book I am reading

Action verb stem + ㄹ/을 + Noun

1. 내일 읽을 소설 a novel which I will read tomorrow
2. 오후에 볼 드라마 a drama which I will watch this afternoon
3. 먹을 음식 food I will eat
4. 선생님께 드릴 책 a book which I will give to my teacher
5. 다음 학기에 택할 과목 a course which I will take next semester

Passive infix

1. 여기에서 산이 보입니다. The mountain can be seen from here.
2. 일년 만에 다리가 놓였어요. In a year, the bridge has been constructed.
3. 아랍어로 쓰였어요. It is written in Arabic.
4. 쥐가 고양이에게 먹혔습니다. The mouse was eaten by the cat.
5. 이 묘지에 묻혔습니다. This person was buried in this cemetery.
6. 밤에 소리가 들렸어요. I heard the sound at night.
7. 창문이 갑자기 열렸습니다. Windows suddenly opened.
8. 가격이 싸서 금세 팔렸어요. Because the price was cheap, it sold quickly.
9. 전기가 끊겼어요. The electricity was cut.
10. 지갑을 빼앗겼습니다. My wallet was stolen (I was robbed).

▌응용 Utilization

1. I like Korean movies.   한국 영화를 좋아해요.
2. My father likes spicy food. 아버지께서는 매운 음식을 좋아하세요.
3. Children like to play online games. 아이들은 온라인 게임하는 것을 좋아해요.
4. I borrowed several books from the Central Library.
    중앙도서관에서 책을 몇 권 빌렸어요.
5. The movie scripts were also housed at the library.
    영화 시나리오도 도서관에 있어요.
6. The movie I saw yesterday   어제 본 영화
7. A fiction book I read this morning   아침에 읽은 소설
8. The place I visited last year   작년에 간 곳
9. An animation I created   제가 만든 애니메이션

10. A laptop computer I bought   제가 산 노트북

11. An iPhone I use   제가 쓰는 아이폰

12. The place where I study   제가 공부하는 곳

13. A café where I go   제가 가는 카페

14. The coffee I drink   제가 마시는 커피

15. The newspaper I read   제가 읽은 신문

16. Due to bankruptcy, the place I was going to live is gone.
    부도가 나서 집이 없어졌어요.

17. I planned for travelling.
    여행 갈 계획을 세웠어요.

18. I am preparing food that I will have for lunch.
    점심에 먹을 음식을 준비해요.

19. The university where I will study   제가 공부 할 대학

20. Courses I will take   제가 택할 과목

읽기 Reading

어제는 재미있는 웹툰을 읽었다.
오늘은 베스트셀러 책을 읽는다.
내일은 인터넷 사이트에서 뉴스를 보겠다.

이번 주의 소설

다자이 오사무 「인간 실격」
단테 알리기에리 「신곡」
무라카미 하루키 「일인칭 단수」
생떽쥐베리 「어린 왕자」
윌리엄 세익스피어 「베니스의 상인」
이광수 「무정」
이지수 「달콤한 기억」
조지 오웰 「동물농장」
파울로 코엘료 「연금술사」

제18과

작년에 갔던 공원 기억하세요?

Visiting

❖ 18. 작년에 갔던 공원 기억하세요?

A 작년에 갔던 선유도 공원 기억하세요?

Do you remember *Seonyudo Park* we visited last year?

B 네. 그럼요.

Yes. Of course.

그 공원에서 오랜만에 고등학교 동창을 만났어요.

At the park, I met one of my high school classmates who I had not seen in a long time.

같이 공부했던 생각이 났어요.

I recall studying with him/her together.

정원에 단풍이 아름답게 물들었던 나무도 생각나네요.

I also recall beautifully colored autumn foliage at the garden.

Seonyudo is an island on the *Han River*, where a water purification plant was located until 2000. Seonyudo Park offers a unique atmosphere with a blend of beautiful nature. Especially in the evening, people can enjoy the night view of the Han River, which is a popular spot for photography.

단어 Vocabulary

작년	last year
갔던	went 가다 to go 갔다 past tense 갔+던 verb ending for past recollection
선유도 공원	*Seonyudo* Park
기억하세요?	기억하다 to remember Verb stem + (으)세요? Polite question form
그럼요.	"Of course."
그 공원에서	At that park
오랜만에	for a long time
고등학교	high school

만났어요.	"I saw/met …"
	만나다 to see/meet
	  만났다 Verb stem 만나 + past tense infix 았
	  만났어요.
	  Verb stem 만나 + past tense 았 + informal polite
	  ending어요

동창을 만났어요.	Met a high school classmate. 동창 literally means alumni. 동창 is a cultural word which reflects a strong social ties based on a person's identity related to schools they graduated from.
같이	together
공부했던	studied 공부하다 to study 공부했다 Verb stem 공부하 + past tense infix 았 (하+았→했) 공부했던 Verb stem 공부하 + past tense 았 + conjunctive for past recollection 던
생각이 났어요.	"Came to my mind…"
단풍	fall foliage
아름답게	beautifully
물들었던	colored 단풍이물들다 colored with autumn foliage 물들다 to be colored 물들었던 Verb stem 물들+ past tense 었+ conjunctive for past recollection 던
나무	tree
생각나네요.	"… thoughts came" "… it came to my mind…"

문법 Grammar

Verb stem + 던 is a retrospective verbal modifier which means "used to" or "had been" recollection of a state of affairs in the past or uncompleted action in the past.

어렸을 때 듣던 노래입니다.
   This song is what I used to listen to.
다니던 학교 건물이 없어졌어요.
   The school I used to attend does not exist.
나의 살던 고향 "Hometown I used to live in"
   (This particular phrase is also the title of a famous Korean song)
읽던 책을 잃어버렸습니다.
   I lost the book I was reading.
부모님께서 바라던 직업이에요.
   Being an entrepreneur was the career my parents hoped for.

Verb stem + 게 verbal noun marker function as adverbial ending

집을 예쁘게 꾸몄습니다. The house has been decorated beautifully.
더워서 얇게 입었어요. Because it is warm, I dressed lightly.
크게 말하지 마세요.   Don't talk loudly.

연습 Practice

Verb stem + 던

1. 울던 아기가 울음을 그쳤습니다. A baby who was crying stopped crying.
2. 여기 살던 사람 아세요? Do you know a person who used to live here?
3. 이 재즈는 제가 자주 듣던 곡입니다. This jazz is what I used to listen to.
4. 제가 먹던 케이크가 없어졌어요. A piece of the cake I had been eating is gone.
5. 작년에 갔던 공원이에요. This is the park I visited last year.

6. 젊었을 때 예뻤던 얼굴은 찾아볼 수 없네요.

I cannot find her once pretty face when she was young.

7. 아버님이 하시던 사업 The business which my father used to do

8. 어제 만났던 분을 또 만났어요.

I saw the person who I met yesterday.

9. 몇 년 전에 헤어졌던 친구에게서 이메일이 왔어요.

I received an e-mail from a friend I parted with several years ago.

10. 지난 주에 갔던 아울렛인데 찾을 수가 없어요.

I cannot find the outlet I went last week.

Verb stem + adverbial 게

1. 이 된장은 자연스럽게 발효되었습니다.

This Korean soybean paste has been naturally fermented.

2. 이 집은 튼튼하게 지어졌습니다.

This house is firmly built.

3. 방을 깨끗하게 청소합니다. I clean up my room nicely

4. 늦게 와요. He/she is coming late.

5. 즐겁게 일해요. I enjoy working.

응용 Utilization

1. This is the tree I planted last year.
   작년에 심었던 나무이에요.

2. This is the café I used to go to last week.
   지난 주에 갔던 카페이에요.

3. This is a song I used to listen to frequently.
   자주 들었던 노래입니다.

4. I found items that I lost.
   잃어 버렸던 물건을 찾았어요.

5. This is the park which I used to visit everyday
   매일 가던 공원이에요.

6. This is the work out exercise I used to do everyday.
    매일 하던 운동이에요.

7. I saw a friend I used to see in the afternoon.
    오후에 만났던 친구를 봤어요.

8. Make it less salty.
    덜 짜게 해 주세요.

9. No man has made a great success.
    크게 성공한 사람은 없다.

10. You should keep your body warm.
    몸을 따뜻하게 하세요.

11. The spring sky looks blue.
    봄 하늘이 푸르게 보입니다.

12. He/she won a gold medal to my surprise.
    놀랍게 금메달을 땄습니다.

13. He/she is smiling in a cute way.
    귀엽게 웃어요.

14. Please stay healthy.
    건강하게 지내세요.

15. Thank you for explaining easily.
    쉽게 설명해 주셔서 감사합니다.

16. Please do not talk loudly.
    시끄럽게 말 하지 마세요.

17. I cleaned neatly.
    깨끗하게 청소를 해요.

18. Can you speak slowly?
    천천히 말씀해 주시겠어요?

19. I arrived safely.
    무사히 도착했어요.

20. I saved steadily.
    꾸준히 저축했습니다.

아름다운 도시 공원

서울에는 공원이 많다. 북한산 국립공원, 한강 공원, 남산 공원, 하늘공원, 서울숲, 여의도 한강공원이 있다. 해외에도 아름다운 도시 공원이 많다. 뉴욕에는 센트럴 파크 공원, 런던에는 하이드 파크, 로스엔젤레스에는 그리피스 공원, 로마에는 팜 플로리 공원, 암스테르담에는 본델 공원, 밴쿠버에는 스탠리 공원, 파리에는 룩셈 브르크 공원이 있다.

제19과

공항에서

At the Airport

❖ 19. 공항에서

A 신지 씨 아니세요?
You are Shinji, aren't you?

어떻게 여기까지 오셨어요?
What brings you here?

B 일본에서 친구가 오기 때문에 마중 나왔어요.
I am here to meet my friend who is coming from Japan.

그런데 연착되었기 때문에 기다려야 해요.
By the way, due to the delayed arrival, I must wait.

선생님께서는요?
What about you?

A 저는 세계일주 배낭여행을 가요.
I am leaving for a backpacking tour around the world.

B 그러세요?
Is that so?

즐거운 여행이 되시기를 바랍니다.
I hope you enjoy the trip.

잘 다녀오세요.
Have a nice trip.

단어 Vocabulary

신지	Shinji, (a male first name) -씨 honorific marker for a person's name
아니세요?	Are you not…
어떻게	how
여기까지	to this place
오셨어요?	Did you come?
일본	Japan
-에서	from
친구	friend
오기 때문에	because he/she is coming
마중 나왔어요.	I came to pick up/meet … 마중 나오다 to come to meet 마중 나왔다 Verb stem 마중 나오 + past tense infix 았 (오+았→왔) 마중 나왔어요. Verb stem 마중 나오 + past tense infix 았 + informal polite 어요.
그런데	by the way
비행기	airplane
연착되었기 때문에	because it has been delayed

기다려야 해요.	"I must wait." 기다리다　　　to wait 기다려야하다　기다리 (아/어/여) 야 하다 "must" 기다려야 해요. 기다려야 + informal polite ending 해요.
선생님께서는요?	"What about you?" 선생님 means a K−12 teacher, however is used when referring to the conversational counterpart in a respectful way.　−님 is an honorific marker.
저	humble form of the first person singular, "I"
세계일주	around the world
배낭여행	backpack travelling
그러세요?	"Is that so?" 그렇다　to be so 그러세요? Due to the ㅎirregular, ㅎ is dropped when adding conjugation. 　　Verb stem 그러 + ending for politely confirming the 　　state of affairs 세요?
즐거운	enjoyable
여행	travel
되시기	nominalizer of the verb 되다 to become 되시다 – Verb stem 되 + honorific infix 시 되시기 – Verb stem 되 + honorific infix 시 + nominalizer기
바랍니다.	바라다　to wish 바랍니다. Verb stem 바라 + formal polite ending ㅂ니다.
잘 다녀오세요.	An idiomatic expression for "have a nice journey."

문법 Grammar

1 Past tense formation

오셨어요? contains the honorific and the past tense infix. There are three past tense infixes: 았/었/였. Depending on the last vowel or consonate of the verb stem, 았/었/였 will apply according to the vowel harmony rule.

오다   to come

오시다   Verb stem 오 + honorific시

오셨다   Verb stem오 + honorific infix시 + past tense였 (시+였→셨)

오셨어요? Verb stem오 + honorific infix시 + past tense였 (시+였→셨) + informal polite 어요?

2   **Verb stem + 기 때문에** is the causal conjunctive ending expresses meaning "because."

날씨가 너무 좋기 때문에 집중이 안 되요.

I cannot concentrate because the weather is too nice.

물건이 싸기 때문에 많이 팔립니다.

Because the items are cheap, they are selling well.

수아는 재미있는 이야기를 잘하기 때문에 인기가 있어요.

Because Sua tells interesting stories, she is popular.

3   **Noun formation or nominalizer**

There are two types of nominalizers. Verb stem + 기, verb stem + 으/음

공부하다 to study	공부하기 studying
걷다 to walk	걷기 walking
듣다 to listen	듣기 listening
배우다 to learn	배우기 learning
쓰다 to write	쓰기 writing
말하다 to speak	말하기 speaking
읽다 to read	읽기 reading
괴롭다 to agonize	괴로움 agony
기쁘다 to be pleased	기쁨 pleasure

만나다 to meet	만남 meeting
밝다 to be bright	밝음 bright
살다 to live	삶 life
쉽다 to be easy	쉬움 easiness
슬프다 to be sad	슬픔 sadness
어둡다 to be dark	어둠 darkness
어렵다 to be difficult	어려움 difficulty
울다 to cry	울음 crying
웃다 to laugh	웃음 laughing
죽다 to die	죽음 death
즐겁다 to be happy	즐거움 pleasure
헤어지다 to break up	헤어짐 parting

4 잘 다녀오세요.

잘 literally means "well" "good"
다녀오다 means "to go and then come back" is a compound verb.
The verb is a combination of 다니다 + 오다 - 다녀오다.
잘 다녀오세요 is a phrase meaning "have a nice trip," or "have a safe trip."

연습 Practice

Verb stem + 기

1. 안경을 쓰면 읽기 편해요.

   If I wear glasses, it is easy to read.
2. 화면이 크면 보기 쉬워요.

   If the screen is large, it is easy to see.
3. 백신 맞기가 싫었어요.

   I did not want to receive a vaccine shot.

4. 졸업하기 전에 인턴십에도 참여할 거에요.

   I will participate in an internship before I graduate.
5. 악기 연주하기가 좋아요.

   I like to play musical instruments.
6. 받아쓰기가 어려웠어요.

   Dictation was difficult.

Verb stem + 기 때문에

1. 비싸기 때문에 살 수 없어요.

   I cannot buy because it is too expensive.
2. 비가 오기 때문에 행사가 취소되었어요.

   Because it is raining, the events are cancelled.
3. 채식주의자이기 때문에 고기를 먹지 않아요.

   Because I am a vegetarian, I do not eat meat.
4. 방이 너무 어둡기 때문에 불을 켰습니다.

   Because the room is dark, I turned on the lights.
5. 충돌사고가 났기 때문에 교통이 혼잡해요.

   Due to a collision accident, traffic is congested.

Verb stem + 아/어/여 야 하다

1. 학교에 가야 해요. I must go to school.
2. 숙제를 끝마쳐야 해요. I must complete my homework.
3. 한국말을 공부해야 해요. I must study Korean.
4. 이번 학기에 졸업해야 해요. I must graduate this semester.
5. 매일 연습해야 해요. You must practice everyday.

응용 Utilization

1. I have to get a job. 취직해야 해요.
2. We have to be careful.   조심해야 합니다.
3. Since it is cold, you have to wear warm clothes.
    날씨가 춥기 때문에 따뜻하게 입어야 해요.
4. We have to wait. 기다려야 해요.
5. Since it is snowing, I will be at home.
    눈이 오기 때문에 집에 있겠어요.
6. Because it is too difficult, we cannot understand.
    어렵기 때문에 이해할 수가 없습니다.
7. Because there are too many mountains, we cannot drive.
    산이 너무 많기 때문에 운전할 수 없어요.
8. That place is too far, we cannot go there quickly.
    그곳은 너무 멀기 때문에 빨리 갈 수 없어요.
9. I should stay here. 여기에 있어야 해요.
10. One should not procrasitnate. 일을 미루지 말아야해요.

읽기 Reading

인천국제공항

인천국제공항은 인천에 있다. 서울역에서 공항 철도를 타면 한 시간 안으로 갈 수
있다. 인천국제공항에는 제1청사와 제2청사가 있다. 세계 각국에서 많은 항공기
가 내리고 뜬다. 공항 내에는 환승객을 위한 시설이 있고 호텔도 있다.

제 20 과

언제 한국에 오셨어요?

Travelling

❖ 20. 언제 한국에 오셨어요?

A 언제 한국에 오셨어요?

When did you come to Korea?

B 삼 년 전에 왔어요.

I came to Korea three years ago.

한국어 공부하러 왔는데 벌써 삼 년이 지났어요.

I came to Korea to study Korean, and it has already been three years.

시간이 참 빨리가네요.

Time is indeed going really fast.

눈 깜짝할 새에 시간이 지나가는군요.

Time passes by like in the blink of an eye.

A 삼 년 동안 공부만 하셨어요?

Did you only study all the time during three years?

B 아니요. 주말에는 국내 여행도 다녔어요.

No. I travelled around the country over the weekends.

A 어디가 가장 인상적이었어요?

Where did you find most impressive?

B 글쎄요.

Well, let's me think.

아, 기억이 났어요.

Yes, I now remember.

해인사요.

Haeinsa Temple.

책에서 읽었던 팔만대장경을 보고 감동했어요.

I was impressed after I saw the *Tripetika* which I only knew from reading books.

단어 Vocabulary

언제	when
한국	Korea 대한민국 Republic of Korea (South Korea)
오셨어요?	"came" with a honorific infix
언제 오셨어요?	When did you come? 오다　to come 오시다　Verb stem + honorific infix 시 오셨다　Verb stem + honorific infix 시 + past tense infix 였 - contracted 셨 오셨어요?　Verb stem + honorific infix 시 + past tense infix 였 →셨 + informal polite inquisitive ending 어요?
삼 년	three years
전	ago
왔어요.	"came" 오다　to come 왔다　Verb stem 오 + past tense infirx았 - 왔 왔어요.　Verb stem 오 + past tense infirx았 - 왔 + informal polite 어요.
한국어	the Korean language
공부하러	in order to study

왔는데	I came but ⋯ 오다 to come 왔다 Verb stem 오 + past tense 았 왔는데 Verb stem 오 + past tense 았 + contrast 는데
벌써	already
지났어요.	time passed 지나다 to pass by 지났다 Verb stem 지나 + past tense 았 지났어요. Verb stem 지나 + past tense 았 + informal polite 어요.
시간	time
참	very
빨리	quickly
가네요.	"⋯going, doesn't it."
눈	eyes
깜짝할 새	in a blink of an eye
눈 깜짝할 새에 시간이 지나가는군요.	Time passes by in the blink of an eye,(indeed).
동안	during
공부만	only study Noun + 만 is auxiliary particle meaning "only"
하셨어요?	Did you do … 하다 to do 하시다 Verb stem하+ honorific infix 시 하셨다하시+ past tense infix였 하셨어요? 하시였+ informal polite inquisitive어요?
아니요	"no"
주말	weekend 주말에는 during the weekend time particle 에 subject particle 는
국내 여행	domestic travel
도	also

다녔어요.	I travelled. 다니다 to get around, to commute, to travel 다녔어요. Verb stem 다니+ past tense 였+ informal polite 어요.
여행을 다니다	to travel 다니다 to travel 다녔다 Verb stem 다니 + past tense 였 다녔어요. Verb stem 다니 + past tense 였 + informal polite 어요.
어디	where
가장	the most
인상적	impressive
해인사	*Haeinsa*, a famous temple located in *Hapcheon*, *Gyungnam* Province.
책에서	in the book
읽었던	Verb stem + 었/았/였 던 connective eneding for past recollection 읽다 to read 읽었다 Verb stem 읽 + past tense 었 읽었던 Verb stem 읽 + past tense 었 + past recollection infix 던
팔만대장경	Tripitaka Koreana
보고서	Verb stem 보 + connective ending 고서 meaning "and" 팔만대장경을 보고서 as I saw the Tripitaka Koreana··· 보다 to see 보고서 Verb stem + 고서
감동했어요.	I was moved. 감동하다 to be moved 감동했다 Verb stem 감동하 + past tense 았 (하+았→했) 감동했어요. 감동했 + informal polite 어요.

문법 Grammar

1 Verb stem + 러 is a connective verb ending meaning "in order to," "to," "for the sake of."

한국말을 배우러 왔어요. I came to learn Korean.
옷을 갈아입으러 집에 갔어요. I came home to change the clothes.
선물을 사러 백화점에 갔어요. I went to a department store to buy presents.

2 Verb stem + (으) ㄴ/는데 is a connective ending used for expressing a transition from the previous action to the current situation.

피곤한데 잠이 안 와요. I am tired but cannot fall asleep.
편의점이 있어서 편리했는데 이제는 불편해요.
Because there was a convenience store, it was convenient but now (since there isn't one) it has been inconvenient.
역에 왔는데 기차가 떠났어요.
I arrived the station but the train had left.

3 Noun + 만 only

문제만 있어요. There are only problems.
밥만 먹어요. I only eat rice.
학원만 가요. I only go *hakwon* (a private learning college preparatory school)

4 가장 is the superlative adjectival marker meaning "the most."

어떤 문제가 가장 어려웠어요?
Which problem was most difficult?
어느 영화가 가장 마음에 들었어요?
Which movie did you like the best?
겨울이 가장 좋아요.
I like winter the most.

5 Verb stem + 고 /-고서 means "… after doing…"

To say that the same one person performs a second action after having previously completed another one, the ending - 고서 to the verb stem of the first action verb while the second verb its sentence-final ending or terminative ending.

요리를 다하고서 창문을 열어요.
After I am done with cooking, I open the windows.
문을 열고서 나가세요.
Please go out after you open the door.
차 한잔 들고서 가겠어요.

▌연습 Practice

Verb stem + (으)러

1. 공부하러 학교에 가겠어요. I am going to school to study.
2. 일하러 미국에 왔어요. I came to the States to work.
3. 여기에 사람을 만나러 왔어요. I came here to meet people.
4. 가구를 사러 왔어요. I came to buy prces of furniture.
5. 편지를 쓰러 책상에 앉았어요. I sat down to write a letter.

Verb stem + ㄴ/은/는 데

1. 이 컴퓨터 좋은데 사지 않겠어요?
   This is quite a good computer. Are you not going to buy this computer?
2. 아직 시간이 이른데 떠나시겠어요?
   It is still early. Will you leave?
3. 배는 고픈데 식사준비가 아직 안 되었어요.
   I am hungry, yet the meal is not ready.
4. 피곤한데 잠이 오지 않아요.
   I am tired but cannot fall asleep.
5. 시간은 없는데 할 일이 많아요.
   There is not enough time, but I have a lot of things to do.

Noun + 만 only

1. 불고기만 먹어요.
   He/she only eats *bulgogi.*
2. 수업 시간에 받아쓰기만 했어요.
   We only did dictation during the class hour.
3. 선생님만 교실에 계셔요.
   There is only a teacher in the classroom.
4. 유니는 수학만 좋아해요.
   Yuni only likes mathematics.
5. 촛불만 켜세요.
   Please light the candle.

가장

1. 어떤 것이 가장 좋은 것입니까?
   Which one is the best?
2. 여우가 동물 중에서 가장 영리해요.
   Foxes are the most clever animals.
3. 형제들 중에서 누가 가장 성공했어요?
   Which sibling is the most successful?
4. 이 가족사진이 가장 소중해요.
   This is the most precious family photo.
5. 이 건널목이 가장 위험해요.
   This is the most dangerous crossing.

Verb stem + 고 /-고서

1. 할 일을 다하고 영화를 보겠어요.
   After I am done with my work, I will watch a movie.
2. 바탕색을 칠하고 다른 색을 칠하세요.
   After I am through with the background coloring, I will paint in the other colors.
3. 휴식을 취하고 일어나겠어요. After I take a rest, I will get up.
4. 경치를 보고 감동했어요. I was moved by the scenery.
5. 소설을 읽고 생각했어요. After reading the novel, I thought about what I read.

응용 Utilization

1. When did you arrive? 언제 도착하셨어요?
2. I came here last year. 여기에 작년에 왔어요.
3. I went to have my car repaired. 차를 고치러 갔습니다.
4. I went to the bank to make a deposit. 예금하러 은행에 갔습니다.
5. Let's go to the park to play. 공원으로 놀러 갑시다.
6. I cannot believe how fast time goes by. 시간이 빨리 가네요.
7. I did a lot of domestic travelling. 국내 여행을 많이 다녔어요.
8. The painting at the museum was very impressive.
   미술관에 있는 그림은 인상적이었어요.
9. I now remember. 기억해요.
10. What country in the world do you like the most?
    세계에서 어느 나라가 가장 좋으세요?

읽기 Reading

팔만대장경 Printing woodblocks of the Tripitaka Koreana

팔만대장경은 경상남도 합천 해인사에 있다. 고려시대 때 1251년에 16년간 걸쳐서
완성한 불교경전의 조판이다. 유네스코 세계 문화유산으로 등록되어 있다. 고려시
대의 발달된 인쇄술과 출판 기술을 볼 수 있다.

스마트폰을 잃어버렸어요.

Telephoning

❖ 21. 스마트폰을 잃어버렸어요.

A 선배님, 스마트폰을 잃어버렸어요.
I lost my smart phone.

인터넷을 사용하고 싶은데요.
I would like to use the Internet.

B 그럼, PC방에 가 봐요.
Then, you might try going to an Internet café.

A 아! 위치 추적이 되었어요. 찾았어요.
Aha! I am able do the location tracking. I found it.

B 다행이네요.
I am glad you found it.

A 미국에 계시는 부모님께 연락해야겠어요.
I should contact my parents in the States.

미국 샌프란시스코는 몇 시일까요?
I wonder what time is it in San Francisco?

B 서울 시간보다 열일곱 시간 느리니까 새벽 네 시이겠지요.
Since San Francisco is 17 hours behind Seoul time, it would be four o'clock in the morning.

A 전화해도 될까요?
Do you think I can phone them?

B 새벽이니까 아무도 받지 않을 거예요.
I would assume that no one would answer since it is early in the morning.

단어 Vocabulary

선배님	선배님 means a person who is senior to the speaker. A noun referring to a person's social status + 님 is a honorific marker. 선배 refers to a student who is senior to a person in college. For example, if a person is a freshman in a department, any sophomore, junior, or senior students will be identified as "a senior" 선배 to the freshman. The opposite word for 선배 is 후배. An upper classmate such as a senior student when referring to a junior year student would say, "1년 후배 이에요" meaning "he/she is one year junior year."
스마트폰	smart phone
을/를	an object particle which modifies verbs
잃어버렸어요.	"I lost it" 잃어버리다 to lose 잃어버렸다 Verb stem 잃어버리 + past tense infix 였 (리+였→ 렸) 잃어버렸어요. Verb stem 잃어버 + past tense infix 였 + informal polite ending 어요.
인터넷	the Internet
사용하고 싶은데요.	… would like to use … 사용하고 싶다 Verb stem 사용하 + conjugation for want, desire 고 싶다.
그럼	"then"

PC방	the Internet café
가 보세요.	"Try going to ⋯."
위치 추적	location tracking
되었어요.	"⋯ it became ⋯," "figure out" 　되다 Verb denoting a process of knowing from an 　　unknown situation. 　위치추적이되었어요. I figured out the location tracking
찾았어요.	"found" 찾다 to find 　찾았다 Verb stem 찾 + past tense infix 았 　찾았어요. Verb stem 찾 + past tense infix았 + informal 　　polite ending 어요.
다행이네요.	I am glad you were able to ⋯.
미국에 계시는 부모님께	to my parents who are in the United States 　미국　The United States 　계시다　honorific verb "to be" 　부모　parents 　-께　honorific particle
연락해야겠어요..	I should contact ⋯
충전	charging
다	all
했어요.	⋯did⋯ 하다 to do 　했다　Verb stem 하 + past tense infix 았 (하+았→ 했) 　했어요.　Verb stem 하 + past tense infix 았 + informal 　polite ending 어요.
샌프란시스코	San Francisco

몇 시일까요?	What would it be? Verb stem 이 + conjugation for probable future ㄹ까요?
서울	Seoul
시간	time
보다	… than …
열 일곱시간	seventeen hours
느리니까	because it is behind 느리다 to be slow 느리니까 Verb stem 느리 + causative conjunction 니까
새벽	dawn
네 시	four o'clock
전화해도 될까요?	Do you think it would be alright to make a phone call?
아무도	nobody
받지 않을 거예요.	… will not answer… 받다 to receive 받지 않다 Verb stem 받 + negative predicate 지 않다 받지 않을 거예요. Verb stem with negative predicate 받지 않 + conjunction for "likely" 을 거예요.

제21과 **스마트폰을 잃어버렸어요.**

문법 Grammar

1 잃어버리다 – Verb stem 잃다 + 어/아 버리다

Korean verbs have many compound verbs. A main verb is supported by the auxiliary verbs. 잃어버리다 originally is a combination of 잃다 (to lose) + 버리다 (to do something completely). 버리다 functions as a terminative auxiliary verb which supports the first or main verb 잃다. The main verb 잃다 means the speaker has lost an item, and 버리다 is as an auxiliary verb which emphasizes the speaker's completed status of what had happened. Thus, 잃어버리다 means "lost something completely."

잃다 + 어/아 버리다

잃어버리다   잃어버렸다   잃어버렸어요.

도박으로 돈을 잃어버렸습니다.   I completely lost my money.
사진을 태워 버렸어요.   I completely burned up the photos.
화가 나서 말을 다 해 버렸어요.   I was angry and I said all I meant to say.

2 Verb Stem + 고 싶다 is for expressing "want to" or "would like to do."

따뜻한 곳에서 휴가를 보내고 싶습니다.
I would like to spend my vacation at a warm place.
맛있는 떡이 먹고 싶어요.
I would like to eat tasty Korean rice cake tteok.
큰집에서 살고 싶어요.
I would like to live in a huge house.

3 Verb stem + -으/ㄴ/는데요 is an ending which implies an uncompleted ending open to a question. It also is for soliciting an answer without directly asking a question to the person. Although this ending is not an inquisitive or a question, the ending intonation is raised.

친구를 기다리는데요.

I am waiting for a friend. (implying "Is there anything else you want to know?")

비쌀 것 같은데요.

It seems to be expensive. (implying "Would you agree with me?")

날씨가 좋은데요.

The weather is very nice. (implying "Maybe we can do something.")

4 Verb stem + 니까 is a connective ending which means "because … due to" and can be replaced with 「Verb stem + 기 때문에」 ending.

커피를 많이 마시니까 잠이 오지 않아요.

Because I had too much coffee, I am not sleepy.

주문하니까 배달 해 주었습니다.

Because I ordered, they delivered it.

카드로 계산하니까 현금은 필요없어요.

Because I paid by card, there is no need for cash.

5 Verb stem + 어/아 도 되다

Verb Stem + -어/아 도 되다 is an ending seeking an approval or asking whether a certain action would be allowed. - ㄹ 까요 is a terminative ending meaning a person is assuming or supposing. The combination of two verb endings means whether the speaker's intent to make a phone call would be adequate.

전화하다   to make a phone call

전화해도 되다. Verb stem 전화하 + conjuction for seeking approval아
         (하+아→해) 도 되다

전화해도 될까요? Verb stem 전화하 + seeking approval아 도 되다 +
         probably future ㄹ 까요?

전화 걸어도 될까요?

Do you think I can (May I/ Can I) make a phone call?

일찍 떠나도 될까요?

Do you think it is acceptable (May I/ Can I) to leave early?

오늘 신청해도 될까요?

Do you think I may apply today?

연습 Practice

Verb stem + 어/아/여 버리다

1. 맛이 있어서 다 먹어버렸습니다.

   It was so delicious, I ate all of it.
2. 헌 옷을 다 팔아버렸어요.

   I sold all my old clothes.
3. 너무 시간이 지나서 잊어버렸어요.

   Since so much time has passed, I completely forgot.
4. 글자가 틀려서 지워버렸습니다.

   I erased all of it because there were incorrect letters.
5. 청소하면서 쓰레기를 치워버렸어요.

   As I was cleaning, I completely cleaned up the trash.

Verb stem + 고 싶다

1. 조용한 시간을 갖고 싶습니다.

   I would like to have some quiet time for myself.
2. 아름다운 시를 많이 읽고 싶어요.

   I would like to read many beautiful poems.
3. 산골에서 살고 싶습니다.

   I would like to live in a mountain valley.
4. 행복하게 살고 싶어요.

   I would like to live happily.
5. 세계여행이 하고 싶어요.

   I would like to travel around the world.

Verb stem + ㄴ/는데요

1. 인터넷이 연결 되는데요. The Internet seems to be connected.
2. 산에서 살고 있는데요. There are people who are living in the mountains.
3. 인삼차를 좋아하는데요. He/she seems to like *ginseng* tea.
4. 잘 모르겠는데요. (You know), I do not know that well.
5. 비가 오는데요. It seems like it is raining.

Verb stem + 니까

1. 어려우니까 공부를 더 해야 해요.
   Because it is difficult, you have to study more.
2. 한국말을 잘 못하니까 주문해 주세요.
   Since I do not speak Korean well, please order for me.
3. 포장을 하니까 예쁘게 보여요.
   As it is wrapped, it looks pretty.
4. 걸으니까 몸이 건강해졌어요.
   Since I have been walking, I got healthy.
5. 제가 로봇 로비에게 물어보니까 대답했어요.
   When I asked questions to Robot Robi, he answered.

Verb stem + 어/아 도 되다.

1. 지금 가도 될까요? Do you think I can go now?
2. 조금 후에 먹어도 될까요? Can I eat a little later?
3. 메뉴를 봐도 될까요? Can I take a look at the menu?
4. 기다려도 될까요? May I wait?
5. 길을 모르는데 물어봐도 될까요?
   I do not know the directions. May I ask for the directions?

응용 Utilization

1. I was too busy and forgot about it. 너무 바빠서 잊어버렸어요.
2. I lost my charger. 충전기를 잃어버렸어요.
3. I spent all my salary for this month. 월급을 다 써버렸어요.
4. I would like to get a good job. 좋은 직업을 갖고 싶어요.
5. I would like to become a medical doctor. 의사가 되고 싶어요.
6. I would like to compete in a *Taekwondo* tournament.
   태권도 시합에 나가고 싶습니다.
7. Why are you asking me? I am reading a book now.
   왜 물어보세요? 저는 지금 책을 보는데요.
8. I searched on the Internet and found it. 인터넷으로 검색하니까 찾았어요.
9. I feel relieved because I was able to do location tracking.
   위치 추적이 되어서 다행이에요.
10. Do you think I can call my friend?
    친구에게 전화해도 될까요?

읽기 Reading

Few phrases from the Movie *Parasite(기생충)*

"그 검은 상자를 저와 함께 열어보시겠어요?"

Would you like to open that black box with me?

"제시카 외동딸 일리노이 시카고 과선배는 김진모"

Jessica, the only daughter, Chicago, Illinois, one-year senior from the same department, Kim Jin-mo."

"아버지는 계단만 올라오시면 돼요."

"Father, you only have to come up through the stairs."

Meaning of Cultural Word 과선배

과 means departments in colleges such as "Department of Liberal Studies," "Department of Foreign Languages." 과선배 literally means a person who is in an upper year or graduates of the same department in relation to the speaker. For example, if a student is in the class of 2023, a student in the same department who belongs to the class of 2022 will be 과선배.

제 22 과 🖊

강의를 들었습니다.

Taking courses

❖ 22. 강의를 들었습니다.

A 오늘은 일요일이어서 차가 많이 없어요.

There are that many cars because today is Sunday.

교수님 강의를 언제 같이 들었지요?

When did we take the professor's course together?

B 작년부터요. 그러니까 일년 동안 들었지요.

From last year. Therefore, we have been taking the course for a year.

A 학점을 잘 받으셨어요?

Did you get good grades?

B 글쎄요. 성적이 좋지 않았어요.

Well. My grades were not good.

더 열심히 공부했어야 하는데.

I should have studied harder.

단어 Vocabulary

오늘	today
일요일이어서	"because it is Sunday" Verb stem + connective causal ending어/아 서
많이 없어요.	"Not many."
교수님	professor, faculty member at a college
강의	lecture, course
언제	when
같이	together
들었지요?	듣다 ㄷ irregular verb meaning to listen or to take a course 듣다 to listen, to take a course 들었다 Verb stem ㄷ is dropped and replaced with ㄹ + past tense 었 들었지요? 들었 + politely seeking another's agreement 지요?
작년	last year
부터	since
그러니까	therefore
일년 동안	for one year
학점	college credit(s)

잘	very
받으셨어요?	"…received?" 받다 to receive 　받으시다 Verb stem 받 + honorific infix 으시 　받으셨다 Verb stem 받 + honorific infix 으시 + past 　　tense였 (시+였→셨) 　받으셨어요? Verb stem + honorific infix 으시 + past 　　tense였 (시+였→셨) + informal polite어요.
글쎄요.	…"well,…"
성적	school grades
좋지 않았어요.	… was not good 좋다 to be good 　좋지 않다 Verb stem 좋 + negative predicate 지 않다 　좋지 않았다 Verb stem 좋+ negation 지 않다 + 　　past tense 았 　좋지 않았어요. Verb stem 좋 + negation 지 않다 + 　　past tense 았 + informal polite 아요.
더	more
열심히	do something hard, assiduously
공부했어야 하는데.	"… I should have studied…" 공부하다 to study 　공부했다 Verb stem 공부하 + past tense 았 (하+았→했) 　공부했어야 하다 Verb stem 공부 + past tense 했 + 　　connective ending for "must" 어야 하다 　공부했어야 하는데 공부했어야 + 　　connective ending for a contrast ㄴ/은 데

문법 Grammar

1 Verb stem + 어/아 서 "because"

Verb stem + 어/아 서 is a causal connective ending which expresses reasons or causes,

오늘은 일요일이어서 차가 많이 없어요.
Because today is Sunday, there are not many cars around.
피곤해서 앉았어요.
Because I am tired, I sat down.

너무 어려서 이해를 못해요.
Because he/she is too young, he/she cannot understand.

2 Noun + 부터 from

작년부터 서예를 배웠어요.
I learned calligraphy from last year.
올해부터 인터넷 강의를 시작해요.
From this year, we will begin online courses.
내년부터 대면 수업을 해요.
From next year, there will be face-to-face classes.

3 ㄷ Irregular verb

Some verb stem ending with ㄷ conjugate regularly or irregularly. Ones that conjugate irregularly are called ㄷ irregular verbs. The stem ending with ㄷis followed by a vowel, ㄷis changed to ㄹ.

ㄷ irregular conjugation

걷다 to walk	걸어요. I walk.
긷다 to draw water	우물에서 물을 길어요. I draw water from a well.
듣다 to listen	음악을 들어요. I listen to the music.
묻다 to ask	물어보고 싶은데요. I would like to ask you.

215

실다 to load   짐을 실어요. I am loading.
깨닫다 to realize   깨달아요. I am realizing.

Here are ㄷ ending verb stems that conjugate regularly.

닫다 to close   문을 닫아요. I am closing the door.
믿다 to believe, to trust   하신 말씀을 믿어요. I trust what you said.
받다 to receive   선물을 받으세요. Please receive my gift.
쏟다 to pour, to put into   정성을 쏟아서 정원을 가꾸었어요.
                           I put my heart into tending my garden.

4 Adverbial suffix - 히

The literal translation of 열심히 is "assiduously." 열심히 includes one type of adverbial suffix is히. A phrase often used "열심히 공부하세요" means "Study hard."

가만히 들으세요. Please listen quietly.
각별히 주의하세요. Please be especially cautious.
도저히 가지 못해요. I cannot possibly go at all.
열심히 공부합니다. I am studying hard.

5 Verb stem + 았(었/였) 어야 하는데 "I should have had …"
This conjunctive verb ending is used when expressing regret for not having done something in the past.

연습을 많이 했었어야 하는데… I should have practiced a lot.
일찍 잤어야 하는데 … I should have gone to bed early.
숙제를 끝냈어야 하는데… I should have finished my homework.

연습 Practice

Verb stem + 아/어 서

1. 바빠서 회의에 참석을 못 했어요.

   I was busy, so I was not able to participate.

2. 늦어서 택시를 탔어요.

   I was late, so I took a taxi.

3. 머리가 너무 아파서 병원에 가요.

   I had a headache, so I went to the hospital.

4. 오늘은 일요일이어서 등산을 가요.

   Because today is Sunday, I will go on hiking.

5. 피곤해서 숙제도 못하고 그냥 잤어요.

   Because I was tired, I simply went to bed without doing my homework.

ㄷ irregular

1. 걷다 to walk

   하루종일 걸었습니다. I walked all day long.

2. 듣다 to listen

   케이팝 음악을 들어요. I am listening to K-Pop music.

3. 묻다 to ask

   한가지 물어보고 싶어요. I would like to ask you one thing.

4. 싣다 to load

   자동차 위에 짐을 실었어요. I loaded my luggage on the roof rack.

5. 깨닫다 to realize

   이제서 깨달았어요. I have now realized.

ㄷ irregular verb stems which do not change

1. 닫다 to close

   상점이 일제히 문을 닫았어요.

   All stores closed at the same time.

2. 믿다 to trust

자신을 믿으세요. Trust yourself.

3. 받다 to receive

이메일을 받았어요. I received an e-mail.

4. 쏟다 to pour

물을 쏟아 부었습니다. I poured out all the water.

5. 얻다 to obtain, to get

이사가는 친구로부터 그릇을 얻었습니다.

I got a set of dishes from a friend who is moving.

Noun + 부터

1. 어제부터 눈이 와요. It is snowing since yesterday.
2. 지금부터 시작합니다. We are beginning from now.
3. 올해부터 온라인 수업이 있어요. We have online classes from this year.
4. 작년부터 바이올린을 배워요. I am learning to play a violine from last year.
5. 내년부터 주가가 올라갑니다. From next year, stock prices will go up.

Adverbial

1. 열심히 연습했어요. I practiced hard.
2. 신중히 생각했어요. thought about it very carefully.
3. 가만히 계세요. Please stay quietly.
4. 집을 찾는 데 정확히 한 달 걸렸어요. It took me exactly a month to find a house.
5. 분명히 말했지요. I told you clearly.

Verb stem + 았/었/였 어야 하는데

1. 시험에 합격했어야 하는데.

I should have passed the exam…

2. 부모님께 잘해 드렸어야 하는데.

I should have been nice to my parents…

3. 한국에 있을 때 태권도를 배웠어야 하는데

   I should have learned Taekwondo while I was in Korea…

4. 더 공부했어야 하는데

   I should have studied more …

5. 심각하게 생각했어야 하는데.

   I should have thought it through more carefully…

응용 Utilization

1. Since last year, I have been learning calligraphy.
   작년부터 서예를 배우고 있어요.

2. From tomorrow, face-to-face classes will begin.
   내일부터 대면 수업을 시작해요.

3. I will study from the basics of mathematics.
   수학 기초부터 공부해요.

4. Because it is cold, I am dressed in layers.
   날씨가 너무 추워서 옷을 많이 입어요.

5. Because I need money, I am working part-time.
   돈이 필요해서 아르바이트를 해요.

6. I borrowed books to read from the library.
   도서관에서 책을 빌려서 읽어요.

7. I walk alone lonely.
   쓸쓸히 걸어요.

8. Please write it exactly.
   정확히 써 보세요.

9. I am talking quietly.
   조용히 말합니다.

10. I should have turned the lights on.
    불을 켰어야 하는데 …

11. We should have been more careful.
    조심했어야 하는데 …

12. I should have brought along an umbrella.
    우산을 가지고 나갔어야 하는데 …

▌읽기 Reading

A public lecture announcement
한글 문화 강좌 팜플릿

매주 목요일 교육프로그램 정보

강연정원	30명
신청기간	2022년 4월 1일 - 2022년 4월 15일
강연대상	주제에 관심 있는 누구나
강연장소	온라인
참가방법	선착순
참가비	무료

여기서 만날 줄은 몰랐습니다.

Meeting People

❖ 23. 여기서 만날 줄은 몰랐습니다.

문화센터에서
At the Culture Center

A 안녕하세요? 치아키 씨 아니세요?
Hi. Aren't you Chiaki?

여기서 만날 줄은 몰랐습니다.
I did not expect to see you here.

B 이번 달부터 요리 교실에 등록했어요.
From this month, I registered for a cooking class.

한국 전통 과자 만드는 것을 배우려고요.
I wanted to learn how to make Korean traditional sweets.

A 취미가 요리입니까?
Is your hobby cooking?

B 네. 음식 만드는 것을 좋아해요.
Yes. I like to cook food.

여름 방학 때 프랑스에 요리 연수갈 계획이에요.
I plan to participate in an overseas training program in France during summer vacation.

유나 씨 취미는 뭐에요?
Yuna, what is your hobby?

독서하고 영화 감상이에요.
My hobbies are reading and watching movies.

단어 Vocabulary

문화센터	Culture Center In Korea, there are learning places or learning annexes called *Culture Center* where they offer many diverse courses for the public.
아니세요?	⋯ are you not ⋯ 아니다 to be not 　아니세요 Verb stem 아니 + 　　polite inquisitive ending(으)세요?
여기서	여기 here 에서 location particle 여기서 is a contracted from 여기에서
만날 줄은 몰랐습니다.	⋯ did not expect to ⋯ 만나다 to see/meet 만나 + ㄹ 줄 모르다 "not expect to ⋯"
이번 달부터	from this month
요리 교실	cooking class
등록했어요.	registered 등록하다 to register 　Verb stem등록하 + past tense infix 였 + informal polite ending어요.
한국 전통 과자	Korean traditional sweets
만드는 것	⋯ thing to make 만들다 to make 만드는 것 　Verb stem + 는 것 (due to the ㄹ irregular, ㄹis dropped.)

배우려고요.	··· in order to learn 배우다 to learn 　배우려고요. 　　Verb stem 배우 + conjunctive " in order to"려고 + 　　informal polite ending요
취미	hobby
요리	cooking
음식 만드는 것	making food
여름 방학	summer vacation
때	at the time
프랑스	France
연수	short-term or long-term educational training program
갈 계획	··· plan to go 갈 계획 　　Verb stem 가 + future modifier ㄹ + noun 계획
독서	reading
영화 감상	watching movies

█ 문법 Grammar

1   ㄹ ending verb

ㄹ ending verbs when followed by consonant ㄴ, ㅂ, ㅅ consonants,
ㄹ is dropped.

만들다 to make　만듭니다 formal polite ending　만드는 Verb stem + 는

놀다 - 운동장에서 아이들이 놉니다.

      Children are playing at the playground.

들다 - 약을 드시는 것을 잊지 마세요. Don't forget to take your medication.

만들다 - 인형을 만드시는군요. I see that ou are making dolls.

Verb stem + ㄹ 줄 모르다 is used with action verbs which expresses "… did not expect …"

만나다 to meet, to see

만나 + ㄹ 줄 모르다 … expect to meet…

만날 줄 모르 + 았다 past tense infix 았

만날 줄 몰랐 + 어요. informal polite ending 어요

만날 줄 몰랐어요.   I did not expect to meet/see you.

비가 많이 올 줄 몰랐습니다.

   I did not expect there would be a lot of rain.

시간이 금세 지나갈 줄은 몰랐네요.

   I did not expect that time would go by so fast.

벌써 대학생인 줄은 몰랐네요.

   I did not expect that you are already a college student.

Verb stem + ㄹ/을 줄 알다 "know how to …."

운전할 줄 알아요.   I know how to drive.

중국어를 할 줄 알아요. I know how to speak Chinese.

영어로 읽을 줄 알아요. I know how to read in English

Verb stem + 는 것 "-ing" or "to do something "

건축 모형을 만드는 것을 배웠어요. I learned making architectural models.

요리하는 것을 배웠어요. I learned cooking. I learned to cook.

사진 찍는 것을 배우겠습니다. I will learn to take pictures.

Verb stem + ㄹ Noun

Noun modifier used with action or descriptive verbs which refer to the future.

연수 갈 계획 a plan to go study abroad and training

공부 할 사람 a person who will study

예약 할 날짜 a date for making a reservation

연습 Practice

ㅂ irregular verbs

1. 벌다 to earn

   돈을 법니다. I am earning money.

2. 살다 to live

   이 곳에서 산 사람 아세요? Do you know a person who lived here?

3. 알다 to know

   어제 아는 사람을 만났어요. I met a person who I know.

4. 울다 to cry

   우는 아이가 있어요.   There is a crying child.

5. 팔다 to sell

   우표를 파는 곳이 어디입니까?

   Where is a place where postage stamps are sold?

Verb stem + ㄹ 줄 모르다 "…did not expect …"

1. 벌써 주말일 줄은 몰랐네요.   I did not expect that it is already the weekend.
2. 이렇게 비쌀 줄은 몰랐어요. I did not expect it would be this expensive.
3. 아랍어를 할 줄은 몰랐어요. I did not expect you would speak Arabic.
4. 이렇게 어려울 줄 몰랐어요. I did not expect it to be this difficult.
5. 할인 행사가 있는 줄 몰랐어요. I did not expect there would be a discount sale.

Verb stem + ㄹ/을 줄 알다 "know how to …."

1. 운전할 줄 아세요? Do you know how to drive?
2. 냉면 만들 줄 아세요? Do you know how to cook *Naengmyeon*?
3. 아이폰 고칠 줄 아세요? Do you know how to repair an iPhone?
4. 불어할 줄 아세요? Do you know French?
5. 공원에 갈 줄 알아요. Do you know how to get to the park?

ㄹ irregular verbs

1. 전화를 걸어요. I am making a phone call.
2. 여기에 사세요? Do you live here?
3. 한 달에 얼마 버셨어요? How much do you earn a month?
4. 울지 마세요. Please do not cry.
5. 집을 팔아요. I am selling my house.

Verb stem + 는 것 "-ing" or "to do something "

1 인형 만드는 것을 좋아해요. I like making dolls.
2. 약 드시는 것 잊지마세요. Don't forget to take your medication.
3. 외국어 배우는 것을 좋아해요. I like to learn foreign languages
4. 피아노 치는 것을 좋아해요. I like playing piano.
5. 우표 수집하는 것을 좋아해요. I like collecting stamps.

Verb stem + ㄹ Noun

1. 다음 학기에 수강 할 강의입니다. It is the course that I will take next semester.
2. 결혼 할 예정이에요. I plan to get married.
3. 걱정할 일이에요.   It is a matter that needs to be concerned.
4. 등록할 과목이에요. This is the course I will register for.
5. 발표할 자료이에요. This is the material for my presentation.

▌응용 Utilization

1. I did not expect to see my Korean instructor.
   한국어 교수님을 뵐 줄 몰랐습니다.

2. I did not know I would meet one of my classmates.
   동창을 볼 줄 몰랐어요.

3. I did not know he/she would speak Korean fluently.
   한국어를 유창하게 하는 줄 몰랐어요.

4. I did not expect that the airplane would arrive early.
   비행기가 일찍 도착할 줄 몰랐어요.

5. I did not know you can drive.   운전하시는 줄 몰랐어요.

6. I found a date for booking a train.   기차 예약일을 찾았어요.

7. He/she has a plan to go for study abroad.   유학 갈 계획이에요.

8. Did you register for a cooking class?   요리 교실에 등록하셨어요?

9. Say to your friend that your hobby is making architectural models.
제 취미는 건축 모형을 만드는 것이에요.

10. Say to a person your hobby is watching movies.
제 취미는 영화 감상입니다.
제 취미는 영화 보는 것입니다.

11. Politely suggest to your father not to forget to take his medication
약 드시는 것 잊지 마세요.

12. I am learning to write screenplays.   각본 쓰는 것을 배워요.

13. Ask a person whether he/she knows how to drive.   운전할 줄 아세요?

14. Say to a person that you are living here.   여기에 살고 있어요.

15. Ask a person whether he reads French.   불어 읽으실 줄 아세요?

읽기 Reading

실외 취미 Outdoor hobbies

야구	농구	보디빌딩	운전	등산	쇼핑	스키	스카이다이빙	스노보드
수영	태권도	걷기	미식축구	축구	야구	비치발리볼	브레이크댄스	
자전거 타기	피겨	스케이팅	골프	유도	라크로스			
럭비	스쿼시	테니스	사진찍기	철도	동호인	배낭여행		

실내 취미 Indoor hobbies

독서 당구 권투 바둑 컴퓨터 프로그래밍 요리 골동품 동전 수집 우표 수집
춤 추는 것 DIY 음악 듣기 악기 연주 영화 감상 요가

제24과 ✏️

이삿짐을 날랐어요.

Moving

❖ 24. 이삿짐을 날랐어요.

A   지난 주에 이사를 했어요.

I moved last week.

그런데 엘리베이터가 수리 중이었어요.

By the way, the elevator was in the midst of being repaired.

B   어떻게 이삿짐을 날랐어요?

How did you move items?

계단으로 이삿짐을 날라서 힘들었어요.

It was hard because I used the stairs.

집을 청소하고 서둘러서 커튼도 달았어요.

I cleaned the house and put up the curtains in haste.

A   일 많이 하셨네요. 좀 쉬셔야 하겠어요.

You seem to be working a lot. I am sure you must need some rest.

단어 Vocabulary

지난 주	last week
이사를 했어요.	"moved" 이사를 하다 to move
그런데	by the way, but
엘리베이터	elevator
수리중	in the midst of being repaired 　전화중 on the phone 　샤워중 in the shower
어떻게	how
이삿짐	personal belongings to be moved
날랐어요?	나르다 to carry objects from one place to another 　In 르 irregular verbs, verb stem 르 is dropped and ㄹ 　is attached to the stem. 나르다 to move 　날랐다　Verb stem 르 is dropped and ㄹ is added. 　　나 + ㄹ + past tense 았 →날랐다. 　날랐어요? 날랐 + informal polite question ending어요?
계단	stairs
으로	by
날라서	because you were moving 　나르다 to move items　르 irregular 　날라서　Verb stem + 라 + 서 connective ending 　　meaning "and" 아/어(라)서

힘들었어요.	힘들다 to be tough, hard, difficult Feeling of tiredness from making physical effort or from having a hard time
집	house
청소하고	청소하다 to clean Verb stem + 고 is connective ending for expressing doing one action after another
서둘러서	in haste
커튼	curtain
도	even
달았어요.	to hang things
일	work
많이	a lot
하셨네요.	"You did..." 하다 to do 하 + 시 Verb stem 하 + honoric infix 시 하 + 시 + 였 (셨) Verb stem하 + honorific infix 시 + past tense 였 하셨 + 네요. 하셨 + Verb ending politely affirming what had happened 네요.
좀	adverb, meaning "a little" used in a phrase politely implying a request or a suggestion
쉬셔야하겠어요.	"(I suggest) you must rest." 쉬다 to rest 쉬시다 Verb stem + honorific infix 시 쉬셔야하다 Verb stem + honorific infix 시 + must 여야 하다 쉬셔야하겠다 쉬셔 야 하 + future infix 겠 쉬셔야하겠어요. 쉬셔 야 하겠 + informal polite ending 어요.

문법 Grammar

1 그런데 is the conjunctive adverbial meaning "by the way" to clarify what is mentioned in the preceding sentence. In the dialogue, the speaker mentions he/she has moved, and is explaining that the elevator was out of order.

사무실 주소로 찾아갔어요. 그런데 이미 떠났어요.

I went to look for the office according to the address. By the way, he/she already left.

지하철을 갈아탔어요. 그런데 틀린 방향이었어요.

I changed the subway line. By the way, I went the wrong way.

그 옷이 어울립니다. 그런데 너무 비싸네요.

That dress looks good on you. By the way, it seems too expensive.

2 르 Irregular verbs

나르다 means "to move items from one place to another" and belongs to 르 irregular verbs. When the 르 ending verbs conjugates in an informal polite form, endings change to 라/러.

나르다 to carry — 날라요.	모르다 to not know — 몰라요
다르다 to be different — 달라요	서두르다 to be in haste — 서둘러요.
부르다 to call — 불러요.	빠르다 to be fast — 빨라요.

3 Verb stem + 고 is used when connecting two clauses with the meaning "and." The topic of either two clauses can be identical or different.

이 태블릿은 간편하고 가격도 싸요.

This tablet is convenient and is also cheap.

불고기도 먹고 물냉면도 먹었습니다.

I ate *Bulgogi* and I also had *Mulnyaenmyeon*.

저는 유학가고 언니는 영국으로 여행가요.

I am leaving for a study abroad program and my sister is going to travel to England.

4   Verb stem + 아/어/야 겠다.

Terminative verb ending meaning "will/probably have to"

빨리 가야겠어요. I probably have to go quickly.
한국말을 공부해야겠어요. I must study the Korean language
기차를 타고 가야겠어요. I have to take a train.

연습 Practice

그런데

1. 전자 사전을 샀어요. 그런데 건전지가 없었어요.

   I bought an electronic dictionary. By the way, it did not have batteries.

2. 눈이 와요. 그런데 길이 너무 미끄러워요.

   It is snowing. By the way, the streets are very slippery.

3. 회장님께서 말씀하셨어요. 그런데 잘 못 알아들었어요.

   The chairperson spoke. By the way, I did not understand what he/she said.

4. 바다에 가요. 그런데 수영복이 없어요.

   I am going to the beach. By the way, I do not have a swimming suit.

5. 목이 말라요. 그런데 마실 물이 없어요.

   I am thirsty. By the way, I do not have water to drink.

르 irregular verb

1. 고르다 to choose

   좋은 것으로 골라서 샀습니다.

   I bought a good item which I chose.

2. 나르다 to move items

   이사짐을 날라요. I am moving.

3. 다르다 to be different

   생각이 달라요. My thoughts are different.

4. 모르다 to not know

   그렇게 어려울 줄 몰랐어요. I did not realize it would be that difficult.

5. 배부르다 to be full

많이 먹어서 배불러요. I am full because I ate too much.

6. 부르다 to call

친구가 불러서 나갔어요. My friend called me so I went out.

7. 빠르다 to be fast

걷는 것이 더 빨라요. Walking is faster.

8. 서두르다 to hurry

응급실에 서둘러서 갔는데 이미 늦었어요.

I rushed to the emergency room, but it was already too late.

9. 이르다 to be early

아직 신청하기에는 일러요. It is too early to apply.

10. 흐르다 to flow

시냇물이 흘러요. A stream is flowing.

Verb stem + 고

1. 어머니는 요리도 하시고 청소도 하십니다.

My mother cooks and cleans.

2. 북쪽에는 산이 많고 공기도 맑아요.

In the north, there are many mountains and the air is clear.

3. 언니는 음식을 잘 하고 집도 잘 꾸며요.

My sister is a good cook and takes care of the house.

4. 이 음식점은 깨끗하고 가격도 비싸지 않아요.

This restaurant is clean and the price of food is not expensive.

5. 유나 씨는 언제나 밝고 명랑해요.

Yuna is always bright and cheerful.

Verb stem + 아/어/야 겠다.

1. 숙제를 빨리 마쳐야겠어요. I should finish my homework quickly.
2. 병원에 빨리 가봐야 하겠어요. I should visit the hospital soon.
3. 점심식사를 해야겠어요. I must have lunch.
4. 이발소에 가야겠어요. I should go to a barber shop.
5. 세탁을 해야겠어요. I should wash my clothes.

응용 Utilization

1. I understand Korean, but I cannot read novels in Korean.
    한국말은 알아들어요. 그런데 소설은 읽지 못해요.

2. I sleep a lot. But I am tired. 많이 잡니다. 그런데 피곤합니다.

3. Bulgogi is delicious. By the way, it is expensive.
    불고기는 맛있어요. 그런데 값이 비싸요.

4. I rushed to the store, but, the doctor was not there.
    서둘러서 갔는데 의사 선생님이 계시지 않았어요.

5. My brother called, so we went together. 오빠가 불러서 같이 갔어요.

6. Walking is good and is also healthy for you. 걷는 것이 좋고 건강에요 좋아요.

7. It is cold and raining. 날씨가 춥고 비가 와요.

8. He/she plays basketball and soccer. 농구도 하고 축구도 합니다.

9. I should reply to my friend's letter. 친구가 보낸 편지에 답장을 해야겠어요.

10. I think I should mow the lawn. 잔디를 깎아야겠어요.

읽기 Reading

이번 주말에는 친구를 만났다. 스타벅스 커피숍에서 만났다. 그리고 물건을
사러 갔다. 세일이 있어서 이것저것 많이 샀다.

제 25과 🖊

매운 음식은 못 먹어요.

Eating

❖ 25. 매운 음식은 못 먹어요.

A 연휴동안 잘 지내셨어요?

Did you have good time during the long holiday?

B 너무 추웠어요.

It was too cold.

오랜만에 친구를 만나서 반가웠어요.

I had good time since I met one of my friends who I had not seen for long time.

그래서 같이 저녁 식사했어요.

So, we had dinner together.

그런데 제가 매운 음식을 못 먹어서 만둣국만 먹었어요.

However, since I cannot eat hot spicy food, I only had Mandu soup.

매운 음식을 먹으면 눈물이 나요.

If I eat hot spicy food, tears come out.

단어 Vocabulary

연휴동안	during a long holiday

지내셨어요?	잘 지내셨어요 is a greeting phrase meaning whether the person has been fine.
	지내다 to spend time
	지내시다 Verb stem지내 + honorific infix 시
	지내셨다 Verb stem 지내 + honorific시 +
	   past infix 였 (시 + 였→셨)
	지내셨어요?
	   Verb stem 지내 + 시 + past infix 였 (시 + 였→셨) +
	   informal polite 어요?

너무	very

추웠어요.	It was cold.
	  In ㅂirregular verbs, ㅂis dropped and conjugates with 우
	  in forming an informal polite ending.
	  춥다 to be cold ㅂ irregular verb
	  추웠다 Verb stem + drop ㅂ + add 우 + past tense었
	   (추우었 →추웠)
	  추었어요. Verb stem + drop ㅂ + add 우 + past tense었
	   (추웠) past infix + informal polite ending어요.

오랜만에	for a long time
친구	friend

만나서	because we met
	  만나다 to meet
	  Verb stem + 서 causal connective verb ending "because"

반가웠어요.	⋯ was pleased⋯ 반갑다 ㅂ irregular verb, to be delighted, pleased 반가웠다 Verb stem + drop ㅂ + add 우 + past tense었 (반가우었 →반가웠) 반가웠어요. Verb stem + drop ㅂ + add 우 + past tense었 (반가웠) past infix + informal polite ending어요.
그래서	therefore, so
같이	together
식사했어요.	⋯ had a meal.
그런데	by the way, however
제	humble form for the first person singular
매운 음식	hot/spicy food 맵다 to be spicy ㅂ irregular
못 먹어서	⋯ could not eat ⋯
만둣국 만두	*Mandu* is a type of dumpling 국 means soup.
만	only
먹었어요.	⋯ ate 먹다 to eat 먹었어요. Verb stem 먹 + past tense infix 었 + informal polite 어요.
먹으면	"if I eat" 먹다 to eat 먹으면 Verb stem 먹 + connective ending "if" 으면
눈물	tear 눈물이 나요. Tears come out.

문법 Grammar

1 ㅂ 불규칙 Irregular verbs

반가웠어요.

Verb stems that end with a final consonant ㅂ conjugates irregularly, and are called ㅂ irregular verbs. However, there are ㅂ ending verb stems that conjugate in a regular pattern.

ㅂ irregular verbs conjugation procedure
ㅂ is dropped and conjugates with 우 in forming an informal polite ending.

반갑다 to be delighted, pleased	반가우 + 어요 — 반가워요. 또 만나서 반가워요. I am very pleased to see you again.
가깝다 to be close, near	가까우 + 어요 — 가까워요. 일본은 한국에서 가까워요. Japan is close to Korea.
고맙다 to be thankful	고마우 + 어요 — 고마워요. 시간을 내 주셔서 고마워요. Thank you for taking time to come.

Following ㅂ ending verb stems do not change.

넓다 to be wide or to be spacious
   아파트가 넓어요. The apartment is spacious.
업다 to carry on the back
   아기를 등에 업어요. I am carrying my baby on my back.
뽑다 to select
   우승 티켓을 뽑았어요. He drew the winning ticket.

2 그래서 "so", "therefore"

매운 음식은 못 먹어요. 그래서 떡국을 먹었어요.
I cannot eat spicy hot food. So, I had *Ttoekkuk*.

세일이 있었어요. 그래서 노트북을 샀어요..
There was a discount sale. So, I bought the laptop.
저를 초대했어요. 그래서 기뻤어요.
He/she invited me. So, I was very delighted.

3 Noun + 만 "only"

만둣국만 먹었어요. I only had *Mandukuk*.
집에만 있었어요. I only stayed at home.
공부는 안 하고 게임만 해요. He/she is not studying but is playing games.

4 「못 + Verb」is an adverbial prefix meaning "cannot." This prefix can also be applied to the ending「Verb stem + 지 못 하다」

I cannot eat spicy hot food.
매운 음식을 못 먹어요.
매운 음식을 먹지 못 해요.

I cannot speak Korean.
한국어를 잘 못 해요.
한국어를 잘 하지 못 헤요.

연습 Practice

ㅂ 불규칙 Irregular verbs

1. 문제가 너무 어려워요. This problem is too difficult.
2. 추운 겨울에는 군고구마가 최고예요.
   During cold winter, baked sweet potatoes are the best
3. 가까워서 편리해요. It is convenient because it is close.
4. 돌이 무거워요. This stone is heavy.
5. 양파를 써는데 매워서 눈물이 나와요.
   While chopping an onion, tears are flowing.

ㅂ verbs that regularly conjugate

1. 어금니가 아파서 씹지 못 해요.

   Due to the toothache in the back (of my mouth), I cannot chew.

2. 아기를 업고 자전거를 타요. I carry my baby on my back and ride bicycles.

3. 대사관이 넓어요. The embassy is spacious.

4. 집이 좁아요. My place is narrow (not spacious).

5. 제인 씨를 회장으로 뽑아요. Let's elect Jane as the chairperson.

그래서 "therefore," "so"

1. 너무 추워요. 그래서 담요를 덮었어요. It was very cold. So, I had a blanket on.

2. 문제가 어렵습니다. 그래서 답을 쓰지 못했습니다.

   The problem was difficult. So, I was not able to write an answer.

3. 시간이 모자라요. 그래서 마감일에 내지 못해요.

   I am short of time. So, I am not able to submit by the deadline.

4. 코로나에 감염되었어요. 그래서 자가격리에 들어갔어요.

   I contracted Covid 19. So, I went into a self-quarantine period.

5. 취직했어요. 그래서 출근해요. I got a job. So, I am commuting to work.

Noun + 만 "only"

1. 만화만 읽어요. I only read comics.

2. 학교에만 있었어요. I only stayed at school.

3. 게임만 해요. He/she is only playing games.

4. 휴일이어서 잠만 자요. I am only sleeping because it is a holiday.

5. 쓰기만 했어요. I only did writing.

「못 + verb」「Verb stem + 지 못하다」

1. 짠 음식을 못 먹어요. I cannot eat salty food.

2. 단 음식을 먹지 못해요. I cannot eat sweet food.

3. 빨리 못 뛰어요.   I cannot run fast.

4. 운전을 잘 못해요.   I cannot drive well.

5. 발표를 잘 하지 못해요. I cannot deliver a good presentation.

그런데 "by the way" or "but"

1. 강의를 시작하는데 그런데 아무도 없어요.

   The lecture has begun, but there is no one.

2. 출발했어요. 그런데 연락이 없어요.

   I left. By the way, I cannot reach him/her.

3. 회의를 합니다. 그런데 자료가 어디 있어요?

   There is a meeting. By the way, where are the documents?

4. 주문했어요. 그런데 배달이 아직 오지 않았어요.

   I ordered, but, the delivery person has not come yet.

5. 공기가 맑아요. 그런데 비가 와요.

   The air is fresh, but, it is raining.

▌응용 Utilization

1. Teacher lent me his/her magazine, so I read them with a great interest
   선생님께서 잡지를 빌려주셨어요. 그래서 재미있게 읽었어요.

2. There are many who got infected with Covid-19. So, only stayed at home.
   코로나 확진자가 많이 있어요. 그래서 집에만 있어요.

3. I crossed the street, so I was able to avoid an accident.
   길을 건넜습니다. 그래서 무사히 사고를 피했어요.

4. Let's help each other.
   돕다 to help - 서로 도웁시다.

5. I cannot eat spicy food
   맵다 to be spicy - 매운 음식을 잘 못 먹어요.

6. He/she carried my heavy lugguage.
   무겁다 to be heavy - 무거운 짐을 들어주셨습니다.

7. I use a light laptop computer.
   가볍다 to be light - 가벼운 노트북을 사용해요..

8. I folded a piece of paper and put it in an envelop.
   접다 to fold - 종이를 접고 봉투에 넣었어요.

9. The classroom is small/narrow.
   좁다 to be small/narrow - 교실이 좁아요.
10. We caught a criminal.
    붙잡다. to catch - 범인을 붙잡았습니다.
11. I cannot cook well. 요리를 잘 못해요.
12. I cannot swim.   수영을 못해요.
13. I studies hard, but I cannot read well.
    열심히 공부했어요. 그런데 잘 못 읽어요.
14. I got angry. By the way, I was able to control my emotion.
    화가 났어요. 그런데 감정을 잘 조절했어요.
15. It was interesting. By the way, I was not able to hold back laughter.
    재미있었어요. 그런데 웃음을 참지 못했어요.

읽기 Reading

한국의 음식

갈비찜 감자탕 김치전 계란말이 꼬마 김밥 닭갈비 불고기 비빔밥
삼겹살 순두부찌개 잡채 치킨 호떡 해물파전

감기가 나았어요.

Flu Recovery

❖ 26. 감기가 나았어요.

A 오늘 좀 쌀쌀하네요.

It is kind of chilly today.

B 어느 계절을 좋아하세요?

Which season do you like?

A 저는 겨울이 좋아요.

I like winter.

B 겨울에는 별로 미세 먼지가 없지요.

In winter, there is not so much "fine micro dust."

B 그럼, 겨울 스포츠를 좋아하세요?

Then, do you like winter sports?

A 네. 스키타기를 좋아해요.

Yes. I like skiing.

주말에는 스키장에 갔었는데 너무 추워서 감기가 들었어요.

I went to a ski resort last weekend, but I caught the flu because it was too cold.

다행히도 금방 나았어요.

Luckily, I got well soon.

단어 Vocabulary

쌀쌀하네요.	"It is kind of chilly today."
계절	season
좋아하세요?	··· do you like? 좋아하다　to like 좋아하세요? Verb stem 좋아하 + polite question form 세요?
저	humble form for "I"
겨울	winter 봄 spring 여름 summer 가을 autumn 겨울 winter
좋아요.	···like 좋다　to like 좋아요. Verb stem 좋 + informal polite ending 아요.
별로	not quite
미세 먼지	미세 means fine,　먼지 means dust 　Ultrafine micro dust which is a dangerous industrial 　pollutant carried by the wind
없지요.	···there are not.. Verb stem 없 + seeking another's agreement 지요

그럼	··· then···
스포츠	sports
스키타기	skiing 스키타다 to ski 스키타기 skiing Verb stem 타다 + 기 nominalizer
주말	weekend
스키장	ski resort
갔었는데	I went but ···
너무	very
추워서	because I was cold
감기가 들었어요.	caught the flu 감기가 들다 to catch the flu
다행히도	luckily
금방	soon

나았어요.	got well.
	낫다 to get well
	나았다 Verb stem 나 (ㅅis dropped due to the ㅅ
	  irregular) + passive tense 았
	나았어요. Verb stem 나 + passive tense 았 + informal
	  polite ending 어요.

문법 Grammar

ㅅ irregular verbs

Verb stems ending with ㅅ conjugates in two ways. One group of ㅅ ending conjugates dropping ㅅ followed by a vowel suffix. Another group of ㅅ ending verbs do not change.

	Verb stem + 어/아 서	Verb stem +(으) 면	Verb stem + 았/었/였 어요.	Verb stem + (으) ㄹ 까요.?
긋다	그어서	그으면	그었어요.	그을까요?
낫다	나아서	나으면	나았어요.	나을까요?
붓다	부어서	부으면	부었어요.	부을까요?
잇다	이어서	이으면	이었어요.	이을까요?
벗다	벗어서	벗으면	벗었어요.	벗을까요?
빗다	빗어서	빗으면	빗었어요.	빗을까요?
빼앗다	빼앗어서	빼앗으면	빼앗았어요.	빼앗을까요?
씻다	씻어서	씻으면	씻었어요.	씻을까요?

☆ 긋다 to draw a line
중요한 부분은 밑줄을 그으세요. Please underline an important part.

☆ 낫다 to recuperate, to get well
병이 다 나으면 여행 갈 계획이에요.

When my illness is completely cured, I plan to travel.

☆ 붓다 to pour
물을 너무 부으면 맛이 없어요. If you pour too much water, it will not be tasty.

☆ 잇다 to connect
점과 점을 이으면 선이 돼요.

If you connect a dot and another dot, there will be a line.

☆ 젓다 to stir
커피에 우유를 넣고 저어요. You put milk in coffee and stir.

☆ 짓다 to build

집을 지어요. I build a house.

☆ 벗다 to take off clothes

더우면 벗으세요. If you are warm, please take off your jacket.

☆ 빗다 to comb

머리를 빗고 나오세요. Please comb your hair and come out.

☆ 빼앗다 to rob

「빼앗긴 들에도 봄이 오는가」

Does Spring come to Stolen Fields is a famous poem by Lee Sang-hwa.

☆ 솟다 to spring out

불이 솟아나서 위험했습니다.

Because the fire spang out, it was dangerous.

☆ 씻다 to wash

집에 오면 손을 씻으세요.

When you come home, please wash your hands.

▌연습 Practice

ㅅ irregular verbs

1. 노란 색으로 밑줄을 그으세요. Please underline with yellow.
2. 병이 다 나으면 집으로 가겠어요. If I get well, I will go home.
3. 전철선이 이어져 있습니다. The train lines are connected.
4. 수저로 저으세요. Please stir with a spoon.
5. 벽돌로 집을 지어요. We are building a house with bricks.

ㅅ verbs

1. 자켓을 벗지 마세요. Please do not take off your jacket.
2. 머리를 빗겨주었어요. I combed his/her hair.
3. 어떤 사람이 제 지갑을 빼앗았어요. Someone stole my wallet.

4. 분수물이 솟아나는 것을 보았어요. I saw spring water surging up.

5. 비누로 손을 씻어요. I wash my hands with soap.

▍응용 Utilization

1. Which season do you like? 어느 계절을 좋아하세요?

2. I like summer sports. 여름 스포츠를 좋아해요.

3. I like drawing. 그림 그리는 것을 좋아해요.

4. I had the flu but I am now well. 감기에 걸렸지만 지금 나았어요.

5. He stole my wallet. 제 지갑을 빼앗았어요.

6. We went to a ski resort but were not able to ski.
    스키장에 갔었는데 스키를 못 탔어요.

7. I studied Spanish, but forgot the language.
    스페인어를 공부했었는데 다 잊어버렸어요.

8. The weather was nice, but it suddenly rained.
    날씨가 맑았었는데 갑자기 비가 왔어요.

9. I am now well because I had an operation. 수술을 해서 다 나았습니다.

10. Underline with red. 빨간 색으로 줄을 그어요.

11. Because I drank too much water, my face got swollen.
    물을 너무 마셔서 얼굴이 부었어요.

12. We are building a large house. 큰 집을 지어요.

13. I wash my hands after coming in from the outside.
    밖에서 돌아오면 손을 씻었어요.

14. I washed my hair and combed it. 머리를 감고 빗었어요.

15. Make sure you stir when drinking lemon tea.
    레몬차를 마실 때 잘 저으세요.

태권도

태권도는 한국 고유의 무예로부터 발달되었다. 오늘날에는 올림픽 종목이기도 하다. 태권도는 손과 발을 사용하는 전신운동이다. 주먹과 손날을 이용한 막기·지르기·찌르기·치기와 발을 이용한 차기 기술이 있다. 요즘에는 태권도와 댄스를 합친 태권댄스가 있다. K타이거즈, 어린이 태권 시범 경기 퍼포먼스는 멋지다.

제 27 과

학기말 시험이 끝나면 등산 가려고 해요.

Farewells

❖ 27. 학기말 시험이 끝나면 등산 가려고 해요.

A 이 컴퓨터 가벼운데요?
This computer seems to be light?

B 네. 새 컴퓨터에요.
Yes. It is a new computer.

무겁지 않아요.
It is not heavy.

메모리가 크고 화상 회의도 잘 되는 컴퓨터를 골랐어요.
I chose a computer which has a large amount of memory and the one that is good for video conferencing.

A 취직 준비하시느라 바쁘시지요?
You must be busy with your job search, aren't you?

B 네. 바빠서 정신 없어요.
Yes. Because I am busy, I feel flustered.

학기말 시험이 끝나면 등산 갈 거에요.
When the final exams are over, I plan to go mountain climbing.

A 어디로 가시려고 해요?
Where are you planning to go?

B 이번에는 설악산으로 가려고 해요.
This time, I am going to go *Mt. Sulak*.

단어 Vocabulary

컴퓨터	computer

가벼운데요?	It seems light (I assume you would agree with me).
	가볍다 to be light ㅂirregular verb
	  가벼운데요. Verb stem 가벼 + 우 + connective for soliciting answersㄴ데요.
	  In ㅂ irregular verbs, ㅂ is dropped, and replaced with 우 when the stem is followed by a vowel.

새	new
무겁지 않아요.	It is not heavy.
메모리	memory
크고	big/large and⋯ 크다 to be big/large 크고 Verb stem 크 + connective ending for "and" 고
화상 회의	video conferencing
잘 되는	⋯ going well⋯ 잘 되다 to go well 잘 되는 ㄴ/는 noun modifier
화상 회의도 잘 되는 컴퓨터	a computer that works well for video conferencing
골랐어요.	"I chose ⋯" 고르다 "to choose" is a 르 irregular verb. In the 르 irregular verbs, 르 in the verb stem is dropped. Pursuant to the verb harmony rule, 라 is followed by 아 and 오 which appear in the stem, and 러 is followed by the stem with 어, 우, 으, 이.

257

	고르다 to choose 골랐다 Verb stem + Past tense formation 라 +았 →랐 Since the verb stem has 오 prior to 르, 라 follows, thus, ㄹ + 았 becomes 골랐다. 골랐어요. Verb stem 고 + Past tense formation 라 + 았 → 랐 + informal polite 어요.
취직	being an employee
준비하시느라	because you are preparing for 준비하다 to prepare 준비하시다 Verb stem 준비 + honorific infix 시 준비하시느라 Verb stem + honorific infix시 + connective ending for causation 느라고
바쁘시지요?	You must be busy, aren't you?
바빠서	··· because I am busy ··· 바쁘다 to be busy 바쁘다 belongs to an으 irregular verb. In 으 irregular verbs, when the last vowel of the verb stem ends with bright vowels 아 will be applied. When the last vowel ends with dark vowels, then 어 will be added. Since 바 ends with a bright vowel, 아 is used. 바빠서 Verb stem 바쁘+ causal connective ending 아서
정신 없어요.	Idiomatic expression for "feeling frustrated." 정신 means "mind" or "spirit." 없어요 comes from 없다 meaning "do not have".
학기말 시험	final examinations
끝나면	when or if it ends ··· 끝나다 to end 끝나면 Verb stem 끝나 + conditional if 면
등산	mountain climbing
어디로	to where
가시려고 해요?	"··· in order to go?" 가다　　　　　 to go 　가시다　　　　 Verb stem 가 + honoric 시 　가시려고 하다　 가시 + intentional connective 려고 　가시려고 해요? 가시려고 + 　　 informal polite inquisitive ending (하+아→해)요?

이번	this time
에	location particle "at"
설악산	Mountain *Sulak*
가려고 해요.	I intend to go.

문법 Grammar

1 Verb stem + (으) ㄴ/은 는데요 can be used both as a terminative or a connective ending. In the terminative case, the phrase implies the speaker's emphasis on his/her opinon on the facts or a status of the object referring to. A close expression in English would be "it seems indeed⋯"

가벼운데요 It (the computer) seems to be fairly light.
반가운데요. I feel very delighted.
아름다운데요. I think it is beautiful.

ㅂ irregular verbs drop ㅂ in the stem and add either 오 or 우.

가볍다	가벼워요.	가벼 + 우 +어요 가벼워요.
	가벼운데요	가벼우 + ㄴ데요.
반갑다	반가워요.	반가 + 우 +어요. → 반가워요.
	반가운데요.	반가우 + ㄴ데요.
아름답다	아름다워요.	아름다 + 우 + 어요. → 아름다워요.
	아름다운데요.	아름다우 + ㄴ데요. → 아름다운데요.

2 Verb stem + (으)면 is a connective ending meaning "if"

취직하면 월급을 받아요.

If I am employeed, I will get paid/will receive a salary.

합격하면 축하 문자를 보내드리겠어요.

If you pass the exam, I will send you a congratulatory text message.

결혼하면 큰 집으로 이사가요.

When we get married, we will move to a larger house.

3   Verb stem + 고 connects to facts or actions meaning "and."

이 컴퓨터는 메모리가 크고 화면도 커요.

The computer has big memory and the screen is also large.

설거지하고 청소를 해요. I do the dishes and clean.

전화를 걸고 이야기를 했어요. I phoned and talked with him/her.

4   르 불규칙 irregular verbs

In the 르 irregular verbs, 르 in the verb stem is dropped. Following the verb harmony rule, 라 is followed by 아 and 오 which appear in the stem, and 러 is followed by the stem with 어, 우, 으, 이.

고르다	to choose
골랐다	Verb stem + Past tense formation 라 +았 →랐
	Since the verb stem has 오 prior to 르, 라 follows, thus, ㄹ + 았 becomes 골랐다.
골랐어요.	Verb stem 고 + Past tense formation라 +았 →랐 + informal polite 어요.

나르다	날라요	짐을 날라요.
다르다	달라요	영어와 한국어는 달라요.
서두르다	서둘러요	문 닫기 전에 가려면 서둘러야 해요.
부르다	불러요	이름을 불러요.
빠르다	빨라요	로켓처럼 빨라요.
이르다	일러요.	지금 가기에는 너무 일러요.
흐르다	흘러요.	시냇물이 흘러요.

5   Verb stem + (으) 느라 is a connective ending which means "because"

취직 준비하시느라 바쁘시지요?
Because you are preparing for a job hunt, you are busy, aren't you?
시험 준비하시느라 고생하셨지요?
Since you were studying for the exam, you must have gone thorugh hardships, didn't you?
운전하시느라 피곤하시지요?
Because you were driving, you must be tired, aren't you?

6   Verb stem + 어/아 서 is a connective ending meaning "because" or "so"

바빠서 정신 없어요.   Because I am so busy, I feel flustered.
밖에 나가서 여기 없어요.   He/she is not here because he/she went out.
피곤해서 쉬겠습니다. Because I am tired, I will take a rest.

7   Verb stem + 려고 is a connective ending meaning "intend to do something."

어디로 가시려고 해요?   Where do you intend to go?
한라산으로 가려고 해요.   I plan to go Mt. *Halla*.
소포를 부치려고 우체국에 가요.
I am going to a post office to send the parcel.

▌연습 Practice

Verb stem + ㄴ/은/는 데요

1. 책이 무거운데요. (Would you agree with me that) This books is heavy.
2. 좀 위험한데요. This seems to be a bit dangerous.
3. 비싼데요.   It seems to be expensive.
4. 맛있는데요. This is certainly delicious.
5. 여기서 먼데요. It seems to be far from here.

Verb stem + (으)면

1. 입학하면 등록금을 내야해요.

   When I enter the school, I have to pay the tuition fees.

2. 졸업하면 대학원에 가요.

   When I graduate, I am going to a graduate school.

3. 빨리 도착하면 연락주세요. If you arrive early, please contact me.

4. 주무시면 깨우지 마세요. If he/she is sleeping, please do not wake him/her up.

5. 아프면 병원에 가세요. If you are ill, please visit a hospital.

Verb stem + 고

1. 서점에 가고 산책을 합니다. I will go to a bookstore and will take a walk.

2. 겨울은 가고 봄이 옵니다. Winter is going and spring is coming.

3. 영화도 보고 등산을 했어요. I saw a movie and climbed a mountain.

4. 천천히 걷고 운동도 합니다. I walk slowly and work out.

5. 좋아하는 일을 하고 돈도 벌어요. I do the work I like and earn money.

르 irregular verbs

1. 맛있는 것으로 골라요.

   고르다 to choose   Choose the one that is tasty.

2. 노래를 불러요.

   부르다 to sing   I sing a song.

3. 전철이 빨라요.

   빠르다 to be fast   Trains are fast.

4. 아침에 가면 너무 일러요.

   이르다 to be early   When you go in the morning, it will be too early.

5. 강물이 바다로 흘러갑니다.

   흐르다 to flow The river flows into the sea.

Verb stem + 느라

1. 영화를 보느라 숙제를 못 했어요.

   I could not do my homework because I was watching a movie.

2. 연구하느라 잠을 못 잤어요. Because I was doing research, I was not able to sleep.

3. 시험 공부하느라 바빠요. Because I am studying for the test, I am busy.

4. 생각하느라 버스 정류장을 놓쳤어요. Because I was thinking, I missed the bus stop.

5. 친구를 만나느라 멀리서 왔어요. Because I am seeing my friend, I travelled far.

Verb stem + 어/아 서

1. 책상이 높아서 불편해요. The desk is too high, so it is uncomfortable.

2. 바람이 불어서 추워요. Because it is windy, it is cold.

3. 그 배우가 연기를 잘 해서 영화가 재미있었어요.

   That actor acted so well, the movie was interesting.

4. 책이 어려워서 이해를 못 했어요.

   The book was too difficult, and I was not able to understand it.

5. 그 곳은 경치가 좋아서 인기가 좋아요.

   Because that place has a good view, it is popular.

Verb stem + (으)려고

1. 무엇을 전공하려고 해요? What are you intending to major in?

2. 점심은 무엇을 잡수시려고 해요? What are you going to have for lunch?

3. K-Pop에 대해서 졸업논문을 쓰려고 해요.

   I plan to write about K-Pop for my graduation thesis.

4. 부모님께 안부 전화하려고 해요.

   I am going to phone my parents to give them my regards.

5. 베스트셀러 책을 읽으려고 해요. I am going to read a best-selling book.

응용 Utilization

1. I really feel I am ill (do you agree with me?). 정말로 아픈데요.

2. This place is small (do you agree wth me?). 여기는 좁은데요.

3. If the streets are congested, let's not go. 길이 복잡하면 가지 맙시다.

4. If it is cloudy, we cannot go. 안개가 끼면 못 가요.

5. He/she has cars and bicycles. 자동차도 있고 자전거도 있어요.

6. I read newspapers and had breakfast. 신문을 읽고 아침을 먹었어요.

7. I chose a good one. 좋은 것으로 골랐어요.

8. They are calling your name. Please answer. 이름을 불러요. 대답하세요.

9. I think it is too soon to recuperate. 회복하기에는 일러요.

10. Leaves are flowing. 나뭇잎이 흘러갑니다.

11. Because I was studying for an exam, I was busy.
    어제는 시험 공부하느라 바빴어요.

12. It took time because I was wrapping the gift.
    선물을 포장하느라 시간이 걸렸어요.

13. I was feeling good, so I sang. 기분이 좋아서 노래를 불렀어요.

14. I am here to apologize. 사과하려고 왔습니다.

15. I am on campus to take an entrance examination.
    입학 시험을 보려고 학교에 왔어요.

읽기 Reading

설악산국립공원

1970년 우리나라에서 다섯 번째 국립공원으로 지정되었고, 1965년 천연기념물로 지정되었다. 국제적으로도 그 보존 가치가 인정되어 1982년 유네스코로부터 생물권보전지역으로 지정·관리되고 있는 지역이다. 설악산국립공원의 총면적은 398.237㎢에 이르며 행정구역으로는 인제군과 고성군, 양양군과 속초시에 걸쳐 있는데 인제 방면은 내설악, 한계령~오색방면은 남설악, 그리고 속초시와 양양군 일부, 고성군으로 이루어진 동쪽은 외설악이라고 부른다. 설악산은 주봉인 대청봉을 비롯하여 소청봉, 중청봉, 화채봉 등 30여 개의 높은 산봉우리가 웅장하게 펼쳐져 있다.

https://www.knps.or.kr

제28과 🖊

늦는다고 문자 보냈어요.

Texting Messages

❖ 28. 늦는다고 문자 보냈어요.

A 늦는다고 문자 보냈어요.
I sent a text message saying I am late.

B 집에서 회사까지 몇 분 걸려요?
How long does it take from your place?

A 지하철 3호선으로 오면 40분 정도 걸립니다.
It takes about 40 minutes by Subway line 3.

광화문 방향 쪽으로는 지하철로 다니기에는 큰 불편 없습니다.
The traffic toward Kwanghwa-gate is congested but it is not so inconvenient to commute by subway.

자동차로 다니면 주차할 곳을 찾아야 하니까 어떤 때에는 시간이 더 걸려요.
If you commute by car, because you have to think about finding a parking space, coming by subway might be more convenient.

오늘 아침에는 자동차로 왔는데 길이 막혀서 늦었어요.
I came to work by car but the road was congested and I was late.

늦는다고 동료에게 문자 보냈어요.
I texted my colleague saying I will be late.

단어 Vocabulary

집	a house, a dwelling
회사	a company
지하철3호선	Subway Line 3
광화문	*Kwanghwa* Gate
방향	direction
다니기	commumting
불편	inconvenience
자동차	automobile
주차할 곳	a place to park
찾아야 하니까	"because I have to find..."
시간이 걸려요.	"It takes time."
오늘	today
아침	morning
길이 막혀서	"because the road was congested"
늦었어요.	"I was late."
동료	colleague
문자 보냈어요.	"I texted."

문법 Grammar

1 Noun에서 Noun까지 "from - to"

학교에서 역까지
From school to the station
청와대에서 광화문까지
From the Blue House (President's Residence) to *Kwangwha* Gate
정문에서 박물관까지
From the front gate to the museum

2 Verb Stem + 기에는 "… turns out to be .."

광화문 방향 쪽으로는 지하철로 다니기에는 불편 없습니다.

The traffic going toward *Kwangwha*-gate is congested, but it is not so inconvenient to commute by subway.

한국어 읽기에는 아직 힘듭니다.

It turns out to be hard for me to read Korean.

여기 살기에는 편리합니다.

This place turns out to be a convenient place to live.

받아쓰기에는 자신이 있어요.

I turn out to be confident in dictation.

3 Verb Stem + 어/아 야 하니까 "because I must …"

찾아야 하니까 불편해요.

Because I have to find the place, it is inconvenient.

빨리 가야 하니까 먼저 나갑니다.

Because I have to go, I am leaving first.

한국말을 공부해야 하니까 다음 주에 만나요.

Because I have to study Korean, I will see you next week.

4 더 "more"

시간이 더 걸려요. It takes more time.

봄이 여름보다 더 좋아요. I like spring more than summer

더 주세요. Please give me some more.

5 Verb Stem + 았/었 (으)ㄴ/는데 "did something but"

This is a connective ending linking a preceding clause expressing a cause which resulted in the following clause

수학 문제를 풀었는데 틀렸습니다.

Although I solved the mathematical problems, they turned out to be wrong.

요리했는데 맛이 없어요. I cooked, yet, it is not tasty.

살을 뺐는 데 아직도 많이 먹어요. Although I reduced my weight, I still eat a lot.

6 Verb stem + ㄴ/는다고 하다 is an indirect quotation verb ending form. Indirect quotes are used when a speaker is relaying a message to a third person.

오다: 오 + ㄴ다고 하다 - 온다고 해요.

늦다: 늦 + 는다고 하다 - 늦는다고 해요.

Minsu says,

"조금 늦어요." → 조금 늦는다고 해요.

"I will be a bit late" → Minsu says he/she will be late.

"자요" → 지금 잔다고 해요.

"I am sleeping." → Minsu says he/she is sleeping.

"전화 해요" → 전화한다고 해요.

"Phone me" → Minsu says he/she will phone you.

"다음 주에 방문하겠어요." "I will visit next week."

→ 다음 주에 방문한다고 해요. Minsu says he/she will visit next week.

"지금 점심 먹어요." "I am having lunch."

→ 점심을 먹는다고 해요. Minsu says he/she is having lunch.

Indirect quotation verb endings

Plain statement	AV+ㄴ/는다고 하다	"늦는다"	늦는다고 합니다.
	DV+다고 하다	"바쁩니다"	바쁘다고 합니다.
	Noun이라고 하다	"의사입니다"	의사라고 합니다.
Interrogative	AV+느냐고 하다	"갑니까?"	가느냐고 합니다.
	DV+(으)냐고 하다	"비싸요?"	비싸냐고 합니다.
	Noun이냐고 하다	"사장님이십니까?"	회원이냐고 합니다.
Propositive	AV+자고 하다	"갑시다"	가자고 합니다.
Imperative	AV+(으)라고 하다	"읽으세요"	읽으라고 합니다.

AV - Action verbs

DV - Descriptive verbs

▌연습 Practice

...에서 - ... 까지

1. 집에서 회사까지　　from home to the company
2. 약국에서 꽃집까지　from the pharmacy to the flower shop
3. 은행에서 마트까지　from the bank to the supermarket
4. 뉴욕에서 파리까지　from New York to Paris
5. 서울에서 제주도까지　from Seoul to *Jeju* Island

-기

1. 아기 돌봐주기는 힘들어요.　It is hard to take care of babies.
2. 공부하기 쉽습니다. It is easy to study.
3. 일하기에는 어렵습니다. It is difficult to work.
4. 악기를 연주하기에는 좋아요.　This is good for playing musical instruments.
5. 흉내내기에는 재미있어요.　It is interesting to imitate.

Verb stem + (이)니까

1. 격리 기간중에 집에만 있어야 하니까 답답합니다.

   Since I had to stay at home during the self-quarantine period, I was frustrated.

2. 이 가구를 사야하니까 돈을 저축해요.

   Because I have to buy this piece of furniture, I am saving for it.

3. 내일 시험이니까 일찍 가요.

   Because there is an exam tomorrow, I am leaving early.

4. 조심해야하니까 천천히 달리세요. Since you have to be careful, please run slowly.

5. 건강해야하니까 운동을 해요. Because I have to be healthy, I work out.

더

1. 더 걸려요. It is taking more time.

2. 일을 더 해요. I am working more.

3. 공부를 더 해요. I am studying more.

4. 산책을 더 해요. I take a walk more these days

5. 더 자요. I am sleeping more.

Verb stem + 았/었/였 는데

1. 비가 왔는데 몰랐어요. I did not know it was raining.

2. 교과서를 읽었는데 잊어버렸습니다.

   I read the textbook but completely forgot what I read.

3. 공부를 많이 했는데 성적이 나빠요. I studied a lot but my grades are bad.

4. 약을 먹었는데 아직도 아파요. I took medication but I am still ill.

5. 아침을 먹었는데 배가 고파요. I had breakfast but I am still hungry.

Verb stm + ㄴ/는다고

1. 늦는다고 동료에게 문자 보냈어요. I texted my colleague saying I will be late.

2. 미라가 도착한다고 해요. Mira is saying she will be arriving.

3. 수연이 영화를 본다고 해요. Suyeon says she is watching the movie.

4. 성진 씨가 쵸콜릿케이크를 만든다고 해요. Sengjin says he is baking a chocolate cake.

5. 선생님께서 소설을 읽는다고 해요. The teacher says he/she is reading a novel.

응용 Utilization

1. I walk from my place to the company. 집에서 회사까지 걸어요.
2. Drawing turns out to be easy. 그림 그리기에는 쉬워요.
3. It is hard for me to see you (implying that the speaker has to make an efforts to see the busy person being addressed) 얼굴보기가 힘드네요.
4. Because you have to go to bed early, please turn off your computer. 일찍 주무셔야 하니까 컴퓨터를 끄세요.
5. I have to clean up my room. Please wait for a little while. 방 정리를 해야 하니까 잠시 기다리세요.
6. It is taking more time. 시간이 더 걸려요.
7. I was on a diet but I am still eating mor. 살을 뺐는데 아직도 많이 먹어요.
8. I slept a lot but I am still sleepy. 잠을 많이 잤는데 잠이 또 와요.
9. I will make more of an effort. 더 노력하겠습니다.
10. The prices went up even more. 가격 더 올라갔어요.
11. It is much colder now. 지금은 더 추워요.
12. He says he can drive. 운전할 줄 안다고 합니다.
13. She ways there are many people. 사람이 많다고 해요.
14. Students are saying they are all busy. 학생들이 모두 바쁘다고 해요.
15. A movie critic says the movie *Future* is interesting. 영화평론가가 "미래"라는 영화가 재미있다고 해요.

읽기 Reading

문자 보내기

□ 안녕하세요? 부장님.

□ 김과장, 갑자기 웬일이세요?

□ 부장님, 지금 길이 막혔어요.
늦게 도착할 거예요.

□ 기다리고 있겠어요.

추석

Chuseok

❖ 29. 추석

A 한국의 추석은 정말 큰 명절인가 봐요.

Chuseok must be Korea's biggest holiday.

서울 거리에 아무도 없는 것 같아요.

There seems to be no one in town.

B 올해는 추석이 좀 일찍 와서 배, 사과가 다 꿀맛입니다.

Chuseok came a little earlier this year. Pears and apples taste good.

늦 여름 참외가 제철을 맞았네요.

Melon is a late summer seasonal fruit.

맛 좀 보세요.

See how it tastes.

단어 Vocabulary

한국의 추석	*Chuseok* in Korea is on August 15 according to the lunar calendar. 의 a possessive particle meaning "of"
정말	truly
큰	big
명절인가 봐요	Chuseok must be Korea's biggest holiday. 명절인가 봐요. Verb stem 이 + connective expressing seems likeㄴ 가 보다 + informal polite ending (보 + 아 → 봐) 아요.
서울 거리	Streets in Seoul
에	location particle
아무도	no one
없는 것 같다	There seems to be ⋯. no/not 없다 to be not 없는 것 같다 Verb stem 없 + connective for "seems not " ㄴ 것 같다 없는 것 같아요. Verb stem 없는것 같다 + informal polite ending 아요.
늦	"late" 늦여름 late summer 봄 spring 여름 summer 가을 autumn 겨울 winter
사계절	four seasons

참외	melon
과일	fruit
제철	in season
맞았네요	in this context means "to receive."
참외가 제철을 맞았네요.	Melons must have come into season.
맛 보다	to taste
올해	this year
좀	a little
일찍	early
와서	because it came 오다 to come Verb stem 오 + conjunction for causation 아/어 서 추석이 일찍 와서 means Chuseok came early. The *Chuseok* holiday which is on August 15 by lunar calendar falls on from September to October depending each year.
배	pear
다	all
꿀맛입니다.	Taste of honey Metaphorical expression of "it is very delicious."

문법 Grammar

1 Verb stem + ㄴ/은 becomes an adjective which modifies nouns.

크다 to be big - 큰 집 a big house
바쁘다 to be busy - 바쁜 학생 a busy student
좋다 to be good - 좋은 소식 good news
중요하다 to be important - 중요한 일 an important matter
가볍다 to be light - 가벼운 책 a light book

2 이다 Copula + ㄴ가 보다 "it seems"

학생인가 봐요. He/she seems to be a student.
휴일인가 봐요. It seems to be a holiday.
명절인가 봐요. It seems to be a major holiday

있다/없다 + 는가 보다 "it seems there are/ there are not"

돈이 많이 있는가 봐요. He/she seems to have a lot of money.
아무도 없는가 봐요.   It seems there isn't anyon.
외국인이 있는가 봐요. It seems there is a foreigner.

Action Verb + 는가 보다
거기에 아무도 없는가 봐요. No one seems to be there.
세탁하는가 봐요.   You/he/she seem/seems to be doing laundry.
마음에 드는가 봐요.   You/he/she seem/seems to be like it.

Descriptive Verb + (으)ㄴ가 보다 It seems/I think
어려운가 봐요. It seems difficult.
피곤한가 봐요. You/he/she seem/seems to be tired.
바쁜가 봐요.   You/he/she seem/seems to be busy.

3 Verb Stem + 아/어 서 Causal connective which means "because" or "since."

늦어서 미안해요. I am sorry I am late.

미끄러워서 위험합니다. Since it is slippery, it is dangerous.

바람이 차서 감기 걸려요. Since it is windy, you might catch a cold.

연습 Practice

Ajectivives

1. 높은 건물은 무서워요. I am afraid of high buildings.
2. 낮은 언덕에 올라갔어요. I went over to a low hill.
3. 초콜릿 케이크는 칼로리가 높은 음식이에요. Chocolate cakes are high calorie food.
4. 작은 물건은 서랍에 넣었습니다. I put the small items in a drawer.
5. 큰 짐은 실었어요. I loaded large luggage.

이다 Copula + ㄴ가 보다

1. 골동품인가 봐요. Those seem to be antiques.
2. 전자 사전인가 봐요. This looks like an electronic dictionary.
3. 작년인가 봐요. It seems to have happened last year.
4. 설악산인가 봐요. This place seems to be *Mt. Seolak*.
5. 이 신발이 등산화인가 봐요. This shoes seem to be hiking boots.

Action Verb + 는가 봐요.

1. 우표를 모으는가 봐요. You seem/he/she seems to be collecting stamps.
2. 문자를 보내는가 봐요. You seem/he/she seems to be sending text messages.
3. 아무도 없는가 봐요. I do not think there is anyone.
4. 김치를 만드는가 봐요. I think they are making *kimchi*.
5. 다음 달에 오는가 봐요. I think he/she is coming next month.

Descriptive Verb + (으) ㄴ가 봐요 It seems/I think

1. 바쁜가 봐요. It seems he/she is busy.
2. 일본에서는 마츠리가 큰 행사인가 봐요. In Japan, *matsuri* seems to be a big event.
3. 불편한가 봐요. You/he/she seem/seems to be uncomfortable.
4. 좋은가 봐요.   You/he/she seem/seems to feel good.
5. 아픈가 봐요.   He/she seems to be ill.

Verb Stem + 아/어 서

1. 싫어해서 마시지 않았어요. I did not drink it because I do not like it.
2. 일찍 일어나서 졸려요. Since I got up early, I feel sleepy.
3. 바빠서 잊어버렸어요. I forgot because I was busy.
4. 공부해서 도움이 되었습니다. Because I studied, it helped me.
5. 포도가 제철을 맞아서 맛있어요. Since the grapes are in season, they are delicious.

▌응용 Utilization

1. It seems New Year's Day and Chuseok are two major holidays.
   설날과 추석이 큰 명절인가 봐요.
2. It seems the weather is nice. 날씨가 좋은가 봐요.
3. It seems prices are going up. 물가가 오르는가 봐요.
4. It seems the Internet is not connecting. 인터넷이 연결이 안 되는가 봐요.
5. It seems the document is missing. 서류가 없나 봐요.
6. It seems everyone has left for home during the New Year holidays.
   설날에 모두 고향으로 가는가 봐요.
7. There seems to be a lot of people. 사람이 많은가 봐요.
8. It seems today is not an exam day. 오늘은 시험일이 아닌가 봐요.
9. It seems to be raining. 비가 오는가 봐요.
10. It seems the cruise ship is leaving. 크루즈 배가 떠나는가 봐요.
11. Pears are now in season. 배가 제철이네요.
12. This fruit is really delicious. 이 과일이 꿀맛이에요.
13. I cooked this. Please taste it. 제가 요리했어요. 맛 보세요.

추석

한국에서 가장 중요한 명절은 설과 추석이다. 설날은 새해를 맞이하는 정월 초하루이고 추석은 음력 팔월 십오일이다. 음력은 보통 양력보다 한 달이나 두 달쯤 늦어지므로 추석은 양력으로 구월이나 시월이 된다. 추석 때가 되면 무덥던 날씨가 시원해진다. 산에는 단풍이 들어 경치도 아름답다. 또한, 추수가 끝나서 곡식과 과일 등이 풍부하다. 그래서 추석은 미국의 추수감사절과 비슷하다고 한다.

제30과

글로벌 한국

Global Korea

A 다음 주는 글로벌 한국 페스티벌이 있지요?
   There is a Global Korea Festival next week, isn't there?

B 네. 연극 공연, 영화 상영, 국악 콘서트 공연이 있어요.
   Yes, there will be plays, movies, and traditional Korean music performances.

   여기 팸플릿 보시면 공연 일정이 나와있어요.
   The performance schedules are available if you see a pamphlet here.

   빨간 색은 연극, 파란 색은 영화, 노란 색은 콘서트이에요.
   Plays are in red, movies are in blue, and concerts are in yellow.

   인터넷으로 예약하실 때 이 QR코드를 쓰세요.
   If you are going to make a reservation, please use this QR code.

   할인이 돼요.
   You can get a discounted price.

A 같이 공연 보고나서 피자 먹으러 갔으면 하는데요.
   I would like to go for pizza after watching the performance together.

B 그러시지요. 좋은 생각이에요.
   All right. It is a good idea.

단어 Vocabulary

다음 주	next week
글로벌 한국 페스티벌	Global Korea Festival
연극	play
공연	performance
영화	movie
상영	screening, showing 상영중인 영화 a movie now showing
국악	Korean traditional music
콘서트	concert
팸플릿	pamphlet
보시면	" if you see" 보다 to see 보시다 Verbstem 보 + honorific infix 시 - 보시면 Verb stem 보+ honorific infix 시 + conditional ending 면
일정	schedule
나와있어요.	"··· is shown" 나와있다 literally means "it is out here."
빨간 색	red
파란 색	blue
노란 색	yellow

인터넷	the Internet
예약하실 때	…when making a reservation
QR코드	QR code
쓰다	to use
할인	discount 할인이 되다 "It is discounted."
같이	together
보고 나서	"after seeing …"
갔으면	if I/you/he/she went 가다 to go 갔다 Verb stem 가 + past tense infix 았 (가+았→ 갔) 갔으면 Verb stem 가 + past tense infix 았 + connective ending "if" 으면
그러시지요.	"Please do so."
좋은	good
생각	a thought, an idea

문법 Grammar

1 Verb stem + (으) 시 + (으) 면

보시면 "if you see"
   보다 to see
   보시다 Verb stem 보 + honorific infix 시
   보시면 보시 + connective "if" 면

2 ㅎIrregular verbs

In ㅎirregular verbs, ㅎ is dropped before a vowel suffix. The descriptive verbs with ㅎin the stem, ㅎ is dropped and the verb stem without ㅎ+ the noun modifier marker ㄴ is replaced.

☆ 이렇다 - to be in this way
   이런 공책은 쓰기 좋아요. This kind of notebook is easy to write in.
☆ 그렇다 - to be in that way
   그런 말씀은 삼가세요. Please do not use words like that.
☆ 저렇다 - to be in that way
   저런 사람이 어디있어요? Where would you find a person like that?

까맣다 to be black	까만 가방 black bag
노랗다 to be yellow	노란 스웨터 yellow sweater
빨갛다 to be red	빨간 볼펜 red ballpoint pen
파랗다 to be blue	파란 액자 blue photo frame
하얗다 to be while	하얀 백조 white swan

Verb stem ending ㅎ remains unchanged

☆ 낳다 to give birth
   새가 알을 낳았어요. Birds laid eggs.
☆ 넣다 to put in
   서랍 안에 넣었습니다. I put in it the drawer.

☆ 놓다 to place

　　탁자 위에 놓으세요. Please place it on the table.

☆ 많다 to be many

　　새해 복 많이 많으세요.

　　An idiomatic expression for "Happy New Year"

☆ 좋다 to be good

　　날씨가 좋으면 나가겠어요. If the weather is good now, I will go out.

3　Verb stem + ㄹ 때

예약하실 때　　　　When making a reservation…

　예약하다　　　　to make a reservation

　예약하시다　　　Verb stem 예약하 + honorific infix 시

　예약하실 때　　　예약하시 + connective conjugation for "when" ㄹ 때

4　을/를　object particle

이 QR코드를 쓰세요. Please use this QR code

엑스프레소 커피를 마셔요.　I am having a cup of espresso coffee.

사진을 찍습니다. I am taking a picture.

5　Verb stem + 고 나서 is the same -고서 ending

When two actions are happening in a sequence, the second action is linked by verb stem + 고 나서

보다 to see

보고 나서 after seeing/watching

아침을 먹고 나서 일하러 갑니다. After having breakfast, I go to work.

일을 하고 나서 이야기합시다.　 After I am done with my work, let's talk.

저녁을 먹고 나서 설거지를 해요. After dinner, I do dishes

연습 Practice

Verb stem + (으) 면

1. 시간이 없으면 그대로 제출하세요. If there is no time, please submit it as it is.
2. 현금이 없으면 카드로 내세요. If you do not have cash, pay by credit card.
3. 공부를 하시면 아시겠습니다. If you study, you will know.
4. 수업이 있으면 학교에 와요. If I have classes, I come to school.
5. 스위스에 가면 스키를 타려고 해요. If I go to Switzerland, I plan on skiing.

ㅎIrregular verbs

1. 빨간 색 드레스 있어요? Are there any dresses in red?
2. 노란 색 가방을 찾고 있어요. I am looking for a yellow bag.
3. 까만 지갑이 있습니다. I have a black wallet.
4. 닭이 달걀을 낳았어요. A chicken laid eggs.
5. 책을 책상 위에 놓으세요. Please place the book on the table.
6. 괜찮으세요? 저는 괜찮아요. Are you all right? I am fine.
7. 싫은 채소가 있어요. These are vegetables I do not like.
8. 파란 볼펜으로 쓰세요. Please write with blue ballpoint pen
9. 하얀 봉투에 넣으세요. Place it in a white envelop.
10. 까만 서류 가방을 찾았습니다. I found a black briefcase.

Verb stem + ㄹ/을 때

1. 예약하실 때 이름을 말하세요.

   Please say your name when you are making a reservation
2. 기분이 좋을 때 아메리카노 커피를 마셔요.

   When I feel good, I drink Americano coffee.
3. 영화가 시작할 때 스마트폰을 꺼 주세요.

   Please turn off your smart phone when the movie begins.
4. 공부할 때 음악을 듣지 않아요.

   I do not listen to music when I am studying.
5. 부모님이 보고 싶을 때 편지를 씁니다.

   When I miss my parents, I write a letter.

Verb stem + 고 나서

1. 연필로 그리고 나서 색을 칠하세요.

   After you draw with a pencil, please paint on it.

2. 휴식을 취하고 나서 대책을 논의합시다.

   After you take a break, let's discuss the solutions.

3. 청소를 하고 나서 창문을 닫으세요.

   After you are done with cleaning, please close the windows.

4. 건강을 회복하고 나서 일에 집중하겠어요.

   After you recuperate, concentrate on your work.

5. 영화를 보고 나서 집에 가겠어요.

   After I watch a movie, I will go home.

▌응용 Utilization

1. I would like to buy that kind of pencil. 저런 연필을 사고 싶어요.
2. Please use the blue pen when writing. 파란 색 볼펜을 사용하세요.
3. Underline with red and highlight with yellow. 빨간 색으로 밑줄을 그으세요.
4. The white dress is beautiful. 하얀 드레스가 아름다워요.
5. The color of the door is black. 문은 까만 색입니다.
6. You have a very good idea. 좋은 생각이 있어요.
7. Please put sugar in the coffee. 설탕을 넣으세요.
8. You do not eat vegetable you do not like. 싫은 채소는 먹지 않아요.
9. There will be series of performance during the Global K-Festival.
   글로벌 한류 페스티벌 기간 중에는 공연이 많이 있어요.
10. The color of my car is red. 제 자동차는 빨간 색이에요.
11. You are looking for a yellow marker pen. 노란 마커펜 어디 있어요?
12. You must wear a black suit.
    까만 색 정장을 입어야해요.
13. Your instructor says to place the book on the desk.
    책을 책상 위에 놓으세요.

14. After seeing the performance, let's go eat pizza.
    공연 보고 나서 피자 먹으러 갑시다.

15. When you are making a reservation, use the discount coupon.
    예약하실 때 할인 쿠폰 쓰세요.

읽기 Reading

K-POP 스퀘어는 서울 강남에 있는 코엑스에 있고 2018년에 개장되었다. 코엑스는 영어의 Convention and Exhibition에서 온 명칭이다. 케이팝 스퀘어에서는 케이팝 뮤직비디오를 감상할 수 있고 광고도 볼 수 있다. 대형 옥외 화면은 감동적이다.

Sample Writing Exercise

오늘

비가 왔다. 날씨가 좋았다. 바빴다. 그래서 시간이 없었다. 한국어를
공부했다. 발음이 조금 어렵지만 배울수록 흥미롭다.

서울

서울에는 지하철 선이 많다. 서울 거리는 복잡하다. 공항에서 시내까지 지하철이
있어서 좋다.

주말

주말에 도서관에 가서 공부했다. 이번 학기는 국제관계학을 공부하고 있고 17학
점 택하고 있다. 오늘은 비가 많이 와서 집에 있었다.

김우주 씨께,

그동안 안녕하셨습니까. 저는 한국어 공부를 열심히 하고 있습니다. 그래서
매일 바쁩니다. 김우주 씨께서도 바쁘시겠지요? 저는 이번 여름에 서울에 가
려고 합니다. 서울에 계시면 만나고 싶습니다. 바쁘시지만 시간을 내어주셨으
면 합니다. 그럼, 이만 줄입니다. 안녕히 계세요.

2030년 5월 10일

A list of nouns, verbs, adjectivals, and adverbials.

❀ **Nouns: 270 Words**

가격	가구	가방	가을	가족	값	강	거리	걱정	결혼식
경주	경험	계절	계획	고민	고양이	고향	곳	공연	공원
공책	공항	과일	과자	관심	교통사고	구두	구입	그림	극장
근처	글자	금년	기간	기분	김치	까만색	꽃	꽃집	나라
나무	날	날씨	남산	내년	내용	내일	냉면	냉장고	년
노래	누나	눈물	느낌	다음	다음달	단어	달	댁	도서관
돈	동대문	동생	뒤	드라마	등산	등산화	라디오	러시아	맞은편
머리	모습	모자	무게	문	문구점	문제	문화	물건	미국
밑	바지	박물관	밖	방	방법	방송국	배	배우	백화점
버스	번호	병원	볼펜	봄	부모	부모님	부분	부탁	분위기
불고기	비	비행기	빵	사과	사람	사무실	사은품	사전	사진
산	색	색깔	생각	생일	생활	서울	서울역	서점	선물
선생님	설명	설악산	성격	소개	소식	손	손님	수업	수첩
시간	시계	시장	시청	시험	식당	식사	신문	신발	아기
아래	아버지	아이스크림	아저씨	아주머니	아침	아파트	안	안경	안내
앞	야구	약	약국	약속	어머니	어제	얼굴	옛날	여자
여행	역사	연락	연필	영수증	영어	영화	옆	오래간만	오랜만
오른쪽	오후	올해	옷	외국인	요리사	요즘	우산	우유	운동
웬일	위	유학	은행	음료수	음식	음악회	의미	의자	이름
이번	이상	인터넷	일	일본	일본어	일요일	자동차	자리	자전거
작년	잡지	장소	저녁	전자사전	전화번호	점심	정리	제주도	졸업
주	주말	주소	주인	준비	중국	지갑	지난주	지난해	지하철
집	찻값	창문	책	책상	청소	축구	취미	취직	치마
친구	침대	카메라	캐나다	커피	컴퓨터	큰형	테니스장	토요일	통장
파란 색	파티	편지	평일	포도	표	품목	피아노	필요	하숙집
학원	한국	한국말	한국어	한복	한식집	할머니	할아버지	할인	행사
형	호	호선	회사	회사원	회의	후	휴일	희망	힘

✿ *Counting Units: 16 Words*

개	권	대	마리	명	번	병	분	사람	살
송이	인분	잔	장	층	통				

✿ *Verbs: 168 Words*

가다	가져가다	가지고 가다	갈아타다	감기에 걸리다	갔다오다	갖다	걱정하다	건너가다	걸리다
경험하다	계획을 세우다	계획하다	고르다	고장이 나다	구경하다	구하다	그리다	기다리다	기억을 하다
기억이 나다	길이 막히다	깎다	꺼내다	끄다	끊다	끝나다	끝내다	끼다	나가다
나오다	돈을 내다	내리다	넣다	노래 부르다	노래하다	노력하다	놀다	농구하다	눈물이 나다
다녀오다	다니다	닫다	대답하다	도착하다	돈이들다	돌아오다	되다	드리다	드시다
듣다	들다	들어가다	떠나다	마시다	마음에 들다	마치다	만나다	만들다	말씀 드리다
말씀 하시다	말하다	먹다	모르다	모으다	모자라다	목욕하다	묻다	물어보다	받다
밥 먹다	배우다	벗다	보내다	보다	부르다	부치다	부탁하다	빌려주다	빌리다
빼다	사고가 나다	사다	사용하다	사진을 찍다	산책하다	살다	서다	설거지를 하다	설명하다
소개하다	수영하다	쉬다	시작되다	시작하다	시키다	식사하다	신다	싫어하다	쓰다
모자를 쓰다	씻다	앉다	알다	알아듣다	어울리다	여행하다	연락하다	연습하다	열이나다
예약하다	오다	오르다	올라오다	우산을 쓰다	운동하다	운전하다	웃다	이사가다	이사하다
이야기 하다	이용하다	이해하다	일어나다	읽다	잃다	잃어 버리다	입다	잊다	잘 되다
잘하다	잠이 오다	잡수시다	전하다	전화를 걸다	전화를 바꿔주다	전화를 받다	전화를 하다	전화하다	조심하다
좋아하다	주다	주무시다	주문하다	준비하다	지나다	지내다	질문하다	짓다	찾다
찾아가다	청소하다	초대하다	축구를 하다	출발하다	취직하다	켜다	콧물이 나다	타다	테니스를 치다
틀리다	푹 자다	피아노를 치다	하다	화나다	회의하다				

❀ *Adjectives: 71 Words*

가볍다	감사하다	계시다	고맙다	공기가 맑다	괜찮다	기분이 좋다	길다	깊다	깨끗하다
나쁘다	적다	낮다	넓다	높다	다르다	더럽다	덥다	따뜻하다	많다
맑다	맛없다	맛있다	멋있다	무섭다	미안하다	반갑다	밝다	배가 고프다	배가 부르다
배고프다	복잡하다	부지런 하다	불편하다	비슷하다	비싸다	새롭다	쉽다	슬프다	싫다
싸다	아름답다	아프다	어둡다	어리다	없다	예쁘다	위험하다	유명하다	이상하다
있다	작다	재미있다	조용하다	좁다	좋다	죄송하다	중요하다	즐겁다	짧다
춥다	친절하다	크다	키가 크다	편리하다	편안하다	편하다	피곤하다	필요하다	한가하다
힘들다									

❀ *Adverbs: 74 Words*

가까이	가끔	가장	갑자기	같이	거의	계속	곧	그냥	금방
꼭	나중에	날마다	너무	늦게	다	더	따로	또	똑바로
마침내	많이	매우	매일	먼저	모두	못	미리	바로	방금
벌써	별로	보통	빨리	새로	서로	아까	아마	아주	아직
어서	안	언제나	열심히	오래	오래간 만에	오랜만에	요즘	이따가	이제
일찍	자주	잘	잠깐	잠시	전혀	정말	제일	조금	조용히
좀	지금	직접	참	처음	천천히	크게	특별히	특히	푹
함께	항상	혼자	혼자서						

❀ *Conjunction: 7 Words*

그래서	그러나	그러니까	그러면	그럼	그런데	그리고

❀ *Question Words: 11 Words*

누구	무엇	뭐	어디	어떻게	언제	얼마나	왜	어느	몇
무슨									

❀ *Numbers: 9 Words*

세	십삼	십이	아홉	여섯	열두	열셋	한	스물/스무	

❀ *Pronouns: 13 Words*

기	그	그것/그거	아무	여기	여러분	우리	거	이	이것/이거
저	저것/저거	저기	저희						

❀ *Determiners: 11 Words*

그	네	두	새	세	스무	아무	여러	이	저
한									

❀ *Interjections: 5 Words*

글쎄요	네	아니요	여보세요	예					

About the Author

Prof. Dr. Maji Rhee is a faculty member at a faculty member at Waseda University, School of International Liberal Studies. Prof. Rhee received doctoral degrees from Rutgers Graduate School of Education and Thomas Jefferson School of Law. Prof. Rhee regularly participates in *Lingua Franca Seminar* and in court interpreting in Korean and Japanese. Major publications include: *The Doomed Empire* (1997), *The Burden of Proof in Transfer Pricing Taxation* (2015), and *English-Korean Dictionary of Criminal Law and Procedure* (2007).

KOREAN

初版発行　2023年2月10日

著　　者　Maji Rhee
発 行 人　中嶋 啓太
編　　集　Sunkyoung Kim

発 行 所　博英社
　　　　　〒 370-0006 群馬県 高崎市 問屋町 4-5-9 SKYMAX-WEST
　　　　　TEL 027-381-8453 / FAX 027-381-8457
　　　　　E·MAIL hakueisha@hakueishabook.com
　　　　　HOMEPAGE www.hakueishabook.com

ISBN　　978-4-910132-38-9

定　　価　2,310円 (本体 2,100円)